*Treasured Memories*
*of a*
*Civil War Widow*

*Sergeant McLain Montgomery*
ARTIST JIM CHRISTY, ROCHESTER, NEW YORK

# Treasured Memories of a Civil War Widow

by

LOIS J. LAMBERT

LITTLE MIAMI PUBLISHING CO.
*Milford, Ohio*
2011

Little Miami Publishing Co.
P.O. Box 588
Milford, Ohio 45150-0588
www.littlemiamibooks.com

Cover design by Steadfast Studios, Mason, Ohio.
Author's photograph courtesy of Shane Gamble, Cincinnati, Ohio.
Cover artwork of "A Promise to Return" by Amy Lindenberger, Civil War Fine Art,
    Gettysburg, Pennsylvania.

Printed in the United States of America on acid-free paper.

ISBN-13: 978-1-932250-89-3
ISBN-10: 1-932250-89-1

Library of Congress Control Number: 2011926613

# Contents

# *Prologue*

*Pray for me dear Mary and if it should be the will of Heaven that [we] meet no more here on earth, remember the cause I battle for is just and look forward to a home where wars never separate and trouble never comes.*
*Atlanta, Georgia*
*July 26, 1864*

---

The letter lay open upon her lap; its pages were well worn and fragile. The words forever locked in her mind were among the last she received from her soldier husband.

She rocked slowly and watched the wrens and sparrows as they settled briefly midst the branches of the mulberry tree off the far end of the porch. She loved this old family home on Dogwood Ridge, and silently congratulated herself on the deci-

*Mary Ann Montgomery*

sion to keep the gnarled old mulberry tree. It created quite a mess from the dropped berries, but it enticed the birds away from the pomegranates and currants that lined the fencerow. Those, along with her prized Queen Anne cherry tree, yielded their fair share of essentials for the jellies, jams, and pies, for which she enjoyed some good measure of respect from her neighbors.

The pipe clenched between her lips gave her small comfort, but offered a distraction to the absence of sound. She was keenly aware that the small child, snuggled beside her on the rocker, cuddled closer while her animated lips moved feverishly. Little Imogene, expecting her great grandmother to answer her persistent questions, peered up into her face expectantly. The child felt hurt and puzzled when the woman neither answered her questions nor acknowledged them.

*Imogene Kinley*

The silence was not a total void, although those around her had long ago given up any efforts to communicate with her through spoken words. They had, with a shrug, acknowledged that she was deaf and thus, forever outside the world of human communication. But this was not altogether true, for there were times, when voices were raised in anger, or intense emotion, that she could follow their words. On those occasions, as on all others, she refrained from any response or acknowledgement and puffed more urgently on the pipe to conceal the pain that arose when the anger and emotion were directed at her.

She had lived a full life, and had faced great adversity, which included the untimely loss of her husband to the battlefield of the Civil War. She had watched her two small daughters grow to womanhood, without the guidance and support of a father whom they never had the opportunity to know or remember. She had forged for herself and her daughters a life full of literature and music while struggling to maintain the family farm. She had opened her home to share the joy of music by teaching the piano to those who wished to learn, and she lovingly passed along her appreciation for books and music to three more generations of women.

Over time, however, as her hearing loss became more severe, she had withdrawn deeper and deeper into her own thoughts and memories. Those memories were like a warm embrace, a safe haven that lulled her gently through the day-to-day tedium of a routine that would eventually lead her to a longed-for release from her silent prison. Her memories were as vivid as if the events had happened only yesterday. She had found that even recollections of painful losses offered solace for they were part of the kaleidoscope of visions that flashed through her mind. Above all, they were not merely images, but were also full of sound and the voices were sharp and clear and filled with emotion. Even the old rocker yielded in her memory a familiar soothing creak in its gentle, repetitive movement.

In her world, the dead were not departed, were not old, but were vibrant and offered welcome company as did the many books crowding the shelves of the parlor of this old farmhouse that she shared with her bachelor brother, James. She found that the works of some of the world's greatest philosophers offered both comfort and inspiration. But most of all, she valued the contents of the well-worn box that held her most prized possession, the letters from her beloved husband,

*Montgomery family home on Dogwood Ridge, Scioto County, Ohio*

McLain. They were her anchor and an ever-present reassurance that the memories she carried in her heart and replayed in her mind, were real.

Her name was Mary Ann Montgomery and she died at age ninety-seven on November 1, 1930, and this is the story of her family as revealed in the letters she treasured so dearly.

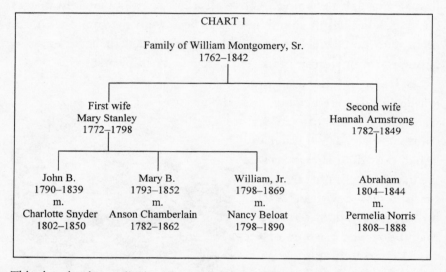

CHART 1

Family of William Montgomery, Sr.
1762–1842

First wife
Mary Stanley
1772–1798

Second wife
Hannah Armstrong
1782–1849

John B.
1790–1839
m.
Charlotte Snyder
1802–1850

Mary B.
1793–1852
m.
Anson Chamberlain
1782–1862

William, Jr.
1798–1869
m.
Nancy Beloat
1798–1890

Abraham
1804–1844
m.
Permelia Norris
1808–1888

This chart has been edited to show only those children who are discussed in the book. Daughters Hannah, Margaret, and Martha of the first marriage are not listed on the chart. Also not listed are the following children of the second marriage: Matilda, Mariah, Melissa, and Milton, all of whom died prior to the beginning of the Civil War.

**CHAPTER 1**

# From Pennsylvania to the Hills of Southern Ohio 1790–1840

## Mary Ann's Story

Mary Ann Montgomery had always been proud of her family's heritage. As with all of the members of her extended family she had learned at an early age that an education was important and that there was no better assurance of a meaningful and successful life than an adherence to hard work, diligent study, and devotion to family. She shared their fierce pride in the opportunities provided in this young country, but understood that fairness and equal treatment of all of its citizens was of paramount importance. Even before she could read, she and the other youngest members of the family looked forward to evenings spent by the fireside with their grandfather, William Montgomery, Sr., who was able to hold their attention in spellbound awe as he recited the details of the family's early experiences. Grandfather Montgomery had the knack of creating vivid images that carried the youngsters back in time as though they too were experiencing and living that early history.

They were proud of the fact that their grandfather, although a fierce defender of his country, bristled at any sign of unjust treatment. To the youngsters, it seemed perfectly logical, even noble, that he had, like so many of his neighbors in Westmoreland County, Pennsylvania, stubbornly refused to knuckle down to the inequitable demands of the tax levied against whisky in the western areas of Pennsylvania. It seemed clear to them that those living west of the Appalachian Mountains were not fairly and equally represented by either their state or national government.

William Montgomery, like his neighbors produced rye whisky, which was shipped to Philadelphia and other eastern cities for sale. When Secretary of the Treasury Alexander Hamilton decided that the best way to pay off the national debt was to collect an excise tax on whisky, tempers flared. Whisky was a primary export of the western Pennsylvania counties. The objection arose from the fact that those counties in which the whisky was produced were taxed on the amount of whisky the farmers sold rather than on the value of the product. The result was that western counties were taxed at the rate of fifty cents per gallon while the tax collected from those buying the whisky was just twenty-five cents per gallon. Tensions ran so high that many feared that a civil war would result as tax collectors were tarred and feathered and western farmers were arrested and jailed. The resistance shown by the western farmers to this Whisky Tax passed in 1791 reached its culmination in July of 1794 when a militia was sent to the area to enforce the tax. It was not until 1802 that President Thomas Jefferson finally removed the excise tax on whisky.

By the late 1790s William Montgomery decided he was fed up with the disputes and what he perceived to be a denial of his rights to fair representation. He packed up his family and began his journey to the hills of southern Ohio. Later, on long winter evenings when darkness descended so early, William would describe for his grandchildren how he and his wife, Mary, along with their five children left their home in Pennsylvania and began the long and dangerous trip following Braddock's trail northwest through neighboring Allegheny County to Pittsburgh where they loaded the family and their possessions on a flatboat and floated down the Ohio. The year was 1798 and

Mary was pregnant with their sixth child. The couple settled near a small tributary of the Ohio River known as Burke's Point where Mary died shortly after giving birth to a son, William Montgomery, Jr.

William explained that their first year was extremely difficult. There were still occasional Indian incursions into the area and there was always the fear that hostilities might arise. He built a home for his young family but he needed help with the care of the children. The eldest son, John, was only eight years old, and the youngest, William, Jr., was just an infant. William hired sixteen-year-old Hannah Armstrong, whose family was living nearby, to help with household duties and the care of the children. Four years later, in 1802, when Hannah was twenty, they were married. The following year was especially significant to the Montgomery family and their neighbors for on March 1, 1803, Ohio was admitted as the seventeenth state of the Union and the first to be admitted from the Northwest Territory.

In March of 1804, Hannah gave birth to the first of six children to be born to the couple. Grandfather William was industrious and determined to build a secure future for his growing family. On March 24, 1813, he purchased an additional eighteen acres, which included the watercourse along Pine Creek, and with the help of his two oldest sons, John B. and William, Jr., he built a dam across the creek and erected two mills. The first of these was a sawmill and the second, a gristmill that was later adapted by his own invention as a press to extract oil from the flax that was produced in such abundance in the area. By 1820 the mills, known as the Montgomery Mills, and later as the Great Oak Mills, were fully operational and had become a popular gathering place where folks congregated to share news of local interest. William had resumed the production of whisky, but had found that the endeavor was more successful in southern Ohio by using corn rather than rye. The sale of his products no longer were transported eastward over the mountains, but were instead floated down the Ohio to the Mississippi to New Orleans for sale. In addition to the mills and their whisky production they not only made their own bricks, nails, and rope, but also raised farm animals and hunted

*Montgomery Mills*
*Along the banks of Pine Creek, Scioto County, Ohio.*

and trapped the native wildlife. During this time more and more settlers came to the area and the town of Wheelersburg, originally called
Concord, was founded in Porter Township, Scioto County. Grandfather William felt strong ties to this community, but was distressed
that the Montgomery Mills were located in Green Township, which
was on the border with Porter. In December 1836, William applied to
the county commissioners to have his land attached to Porter Township. Accordingly, on December 7, the border was moved to include
the Montgomery property on Dogwood Ridge and the mills on Pine
Creek.

## Good Times and Bad

The 1830s brought even more changes to the Montgomery family and
to their neighbors in southern Ohio. By then, the five oldest children
of William Montgomery had married and started families of their
own. Eighteen thirty-two was especially significant in that it was the
year that Mary Ann was born to William Montgomery, Jr., and his
wife Nancy, and also the year that her cousin McLain was born to

John B. Montgomery and his wife Charlotte. No one could have foreseen the inexorable bond that would be formed between the two cousins.

Mary Ann and her siblings and cousins were often reminded that their own lives were far more pleasant and comfortable than that of their grandparents and parents who had faced so many hardships. They tried to imagine how different the 150-acre tract of land, in what was known as the French Grant, on Dogwood Ridge along the banks of Pine Creek, would have been with nothing but forests covering the land. They felt lucky that they had been spared the hard work necessary to transform it into the prosperous and comfortable home they enjoyed.

The area was destined to benefit from a new prosperity as technology and transportation improvements were developed that linked the area to other parts of the state. The Ohio and Erie Canal system, for example, completed in 1832, followed the course of the Scioto River from Columbus to Portsmouth on the banks of the Ohio. As with all innovations there are often unforeseen consequences. It was perhaps no coincidence that the dreaded disease cholera struck the area in the fall of that same year. The illness produced severe vomiting and diarrhea resulting in dehydration and often proved deadly within hours after the first appearance of symptoms. Drinking water and food contaminated with human feces caused the disease; however, the source of the illness was a mystery at the time. Antibiotics were unknown, but some well-meaning doctors treated the disease with calomel, which contained mercury, causing hundreds who might have survived the initial disease to succumb to mercury poisoning. The Montgomery family, like their neighbors, feared for the welfare of themselves and their children and, indeed, some fell victim to the disease.

The canals were also often the source of stagnant water that served as a breeding ground for malaria carrying mosquitoes. Even the rivers, which routinely overflowed their banks in the springtime, flooded the bottomlands depositing yearly layers of silt, which, although providing fertile ground for crops, also yielded their fair share of illness. People became understandably frightened by these mysterious diseases and often mistakenly assumed that any illness, no matter how mild, was cholera if symptoms included vomiting and diarrhea.

In addition to health issues, the area was also affected, along with the rest of the country, by the Panic of 1837. The word "panic," which was used to refer to an economic downturn, has been replaced today by the less alarming words "recession" or the more serious "depression." It was not until 1843 that the country had fully recovered from the economic slump that had resulted in closed banks, loss of life savings, and a national unemployment rate of nearly ten percent. Although the impact was felt throughout the country, large cities suffered most. The Montgomery family and their neighbors were fortunate that Scioto County seemed to weather the economic storms of 1837, as well as the later downturn of 1857, better than many others.

Another significant factor for the local economy was the strong influx of Welsh immigrants into Ohio in the mid-1830s. Those who settled in the lower Scioto Valley brought with them the knowledge of how best to exploit the coal, iron ore, limestone, and timber resources that were so abundant there. They built blast furnaces in which they melted the ore and created various items of solid iron. Scioto County and neighboring Ohio counties of Jackson, Vinton, and Lawrence as well as the Kentucky counties of Greenup, Boyd, Carter, and Lewis were known worldwide for the quality of the iron produced in a thirty-mile stretch referred to as the Hanging Rock region.

## *The Allure of the Charismatic Mr. Reeve*

Midst all of the many changes occurring in and around Wheelersburg, the first chink in the seemingly impenetrable armor of the close-knit family occurred in 1838. In a surprising turn of events, gregarious and headstrong Albina Montgomery decided to leave Ohio for the unknown lands of northern Illinois. She planned to join a party of adventurous pioneers led by Orange County, New York, native Tracy Reeve, Jr.

The family of Tracy Reeve, Sr., had come to Ohio in 1814 and eventually settled in Scioto County; however, his son, an energetic and enterprising young man was eager to pursue his own fortune and was drawn by the appeal of western lands. In May of 1834, he traveled to Bureau County, Illinois, where he acquired 240 acres of land and then returned to Ohio in 1836. Upon his return, he extolled the virtues of the prairie and of the opportunities available there. He spoke of the heroic efforts of the Illinois Militia and the regular army in their efforts to free the land from Indian attack during the Black Hawk War, and assured his Ohio friends that the new frontier was finally safe. As proof of his claims, he entertained them with tales of his encounters with the famous Pottawatomie chief Shabbona, a true friend of the white man, and assured them that the northern prairie lands of Illinois were at last free of any threat from hostile Indians.

In April of that year, the young land speculator organized a small party of venturesome souls and took the group to Bureau County. There, he laid out a town, which he called Greenfield, and began to sell lots. Since there was already a town by that name, the Illinois legislature later changed the name to LaMoille.

The soil of the prairie proved to be ideal for farming and also provided a bounty of wildlife that lured hunters as well as farmers. So enthusiastic were the reports from these most recent pioneers that Reeve returned to Scioto County in 1838 and again recruited others to join him in Illinois. Among those who initially expressed some interest in Reeve's proposal was the family of John B. Montgomery. John's wife, Charlotte, however was adamant that the family remain together among friends and relatives in southern Ohio. Her request was accepted and honored by all except oldest daughter, sixteen-year-old Albina, who was determined to join the group bound for Illinois. It is difficult to understand how her parents could have permitted the young girl to leave her family and travel to this fearsome and unknown location. Perhaps it was her own wild spirit for adventure that lured her. But most likely it was the captivating charm of Tracy Reeve, Jr., the handsome, charismatic, young bachelor, that enticed young Albina. Whatever the reason, she had stubbornly insisted that she would accompany the group as a hired girl to the Reeve household. Against her family's wishes, she left for Illinois.

Young Albina Montgomery worked as a servant in the Reeve home for a year and a half before leaving LaMoille. If Albina had entertained any romantic ideas regarding her employer, her hopes would have been dashed upon the realization that the charming Mr. Reeve enjoyed the company of a steady stream of attractive young women who were employed in his household. After spending a year and a half in the Reeve household, Albina realized that there was no future for her there. She moved to the nearby town of Princeton where she met her future husband, Alexander Hamilton Janes, married, and started a family of her own.

## *The Ohio Legacy of Grandfather William Montgomery, Sr.*

Meanwhile, at home in Ohio, there were many changes in store for the family. Grandfather William had excelled in every economic venture he undertook and he looked forward to the day when his sons would embrace this inheritance and continue his efforts to ensure future economic advantages for the family. But, apparently, neither of the two sons who had helped him build the mills shared his enthusiasm for that occupation.

Eldest son, John B., loved to hunt and valued the freedom to enjoy his passions without the daily constraints of running a business. Younger brother William, Jr., was a successful farmer, but he too, disliked being tied to administrative details and tedious record keeping. Both brothers had been more than happy to relinquish their responsibilities at the mills to their brother-in-law, Anson B. Chamberlain, who had married their sister Mary.

Anson was well respected in the community and seemed to enjoy running the mills while maintaining his own farm. Probably it was the social prominence of the mills that appealed to him most. He never tired of entertaining visitors to the mill with his stories about his service in the War of 1812. He had served as a private in Captain William Huston's mounted company of Ohio Militia; however, some twenty years after the fact, his stories had acquired a life and reality of their own. Folks liked Anson and admired his capabilities and were more than happy to bestow upon him the honorary title of "major."

Tragedy struck the family in the summer of 1839 with the disappearance and presumed death of William's eldest son, John. Although only seven years old at the time, Mary Ann was aware of the veiled comments and whispered conversation regarding the disappearance of her uncle. Mystery and rumor provided no decisive evidence regarding his fate; however, Mary Ann and her siblings and cousins were assured that he most probably drowned while hunting. But the disturbing fact remained that there was no conclusive evidence regarding his disappearance, nor was his body ever found.

William was distraught at the news regarding his son and his own health seemed to decline. In August of that same year at age seventy-two, he and his wife Hannah sold the mills to their heirs. Accordingly, ownership of the Montgomery Mills was transferred to their surviving children and to the children of their deceased son, John, for the sum of two thousand dollars. As before, the day-to-day operation of the mills remained in the capable hands of Anson Chamberlain as William's health continued to decline. William Montgomery, Sr., died on October 5, 1842, at age seventy-five.

The family suffered a number of losses from the late thirties through the 1840s. In addition to eldest son, John, and grandfather, William, five other family members, including grandmother, Hannah, as well as sons Milton and Abraham and daughters Matilda and Mariah, died from disease. The deadly effects of the dreaded cholera as well as the highly contagious tuberculosis were visited upon them. The loss of so many family members produced a dramatic change in the family dynamics for those in Ohio. Perhaps it was the enormity of their loss coupled with the perception that the climate of southern Ohio was unhealthy since John's widow, Charlotte, was already showing signs of tuberculosis. Whatever their motivation, the widow and her children decided to move west. The obvious choice was to join Albina in Illinois where things were looking up for the young girl.

On June 30, 1841, nineteen-year-old Albina married thirty-year-old Massachusetts native, Alexander Hamilton Janes and the couple moved to the village of Walnut in Bureau County.

Albina had repeatedly encouraged her mother and siblings to join her and her husband in Illinois. In 1844, after the spring thaw, Albina and her husband traveled to Scioto County to attend to financial matters and to visit with the family. On April 2, 1844, they sold Albina's inherited share of her father's estate. On April 3, her older brother John sold his property and, three days later, her mother, Charlotte, sold her share of real estate as well. The widow, Charlotte, and her children left Dogwood Ridge, the mills, their uncle William and aunt Nancy, and their ten cousins and moved west to what they hoped would be a more healthful climate. It was a tearful day for everyone as they promised to write often and to never forget their loved ones in southern Ohio. Twelve-year-old Mary Ann was particularly sad that day and felt that the loss was almost too much to bear. Her mother, Nancy assured her that family ties were too strong to be severed by distance. It became a routine for Nancy and her daughters to read the names of the descendants of William Montgomery, Sr., recorded in the old family Bible, and in turn, to recount a favorite story about happy events shared by the family in earlier days. It was their solemn, unspoken oath that these family members would never be forgotten.

**CHAPTER 2**

# The Prairie Lands of Northern Illinois 1830–1860

## Life on the Prairie

During the spring of 1844 when Albina briefly returned to Scioto County, she had entertained her young cousins with stories about life on the prairie. When Aunt Charlotte and her children left Ohio to join Albina in Bureau County, those left behind beseeched them to write on a regular basis and assured them that even the smallest detail of their lives would be of interest. Mary Ann and her family eagerly awaited the arrival of any and all letters regarding their relatives in Illinois.

In her first letter to the folks in Ohio, Aunt Charlotte confided that she had based her expectations of their new home upon the glowing reports she had received from Albina. As twelve-year-old Mary Ann listened while her mother read the letter, she shuddered at the gloomy descriptions of flat sprawling grasslands and low-lying swamps and the bitterly cold winters which produced ice choked streams and rivers. Charlotte also revealed that her hopes for improved health had been dashed. The violent coughing attacks from her tuberculosis had become more frequent and more severe, but she had found a good doctor who had prescribed laudanum, which gave her some comfort. Mary Ann, who was no fan of cold wintry weather, decided that it must be a truly terrible place. The nearby Scioto River occasionally froze, but Mary Ann couldn't recall a time that the mighty Ohio River was frozen to the point where boats could not navigate it until spring. Her aunt Charlotte had admitted that their new home in Bureau County was still part of the frontier and certainly was not experiencing the kind of economic boom they had enjoyed in the hills of southern Ohio. She also acknowledged that the northern part of the state where they had settled was viewed by many as being less desirable than the southern portions of the state. Mary Ann concluded that Aunt Charlotte had some misgivings about her decision to follow Albina and her husband to Illinois.

Although Mary Ann and her siblings had initially been disappointed that they too had not been among the daring souls who had traveled to this new and unknown land, their views of the prairie were far less optimistic upon learning of the desolate conditions there. However each new letter from Illinois filled their imaginations with exotic images of adventure. When cousin Albina wrote of her own experiences with the famed Indian chief Shabbona they were intrigued and once again felt a bit envious.

## The Black Hawk War

Mary Ann remembered listening to the stories told by Tracy Reeve as he captivated his audiences in Scioto County with stories about how the prairie had been freed from Indian attack and was finally safe for settlement. She recalled his tales of the problems caused by Chief Black Hawk and of how the friendly Chief Shabbona and the Illinois Militia had successfully rid the area of hostile Indians and saved the lives of the settlers. When Albina revealed that she and her husband actually knew the chief and often entertained Chief Shabbona and his wife in their home, Mary Ann and her siblings were doubly impressed and eagerly awaited each of her letters to learn more.

They were never disappointed for Albina was delighted to relay details about her many visits with Shabbona. The old chief was an enthusiastic storyteller and loved to entertain the settlers with tales of his relationship with Chief Black Hawk. Albina had a way with words herself and wrote such lively, detailed accounts that Mary Ann and her siblings felt that they had been witness to the events. A favorite activity for Mary Ann and her sisters, Cynthia and Sarah, and brothers, George and James, was to re-enact the stories sent by Albina and to entertain their family and friends with their own dramatic presentations. George, being the older male, insisted upon playing the role of the hero, Chief Shabbona, and dressed himself with deerskin leggings and feathers for his hair. Younger brother James was relegated to play the villain, Black Hawk. Mary Ann was actually content to permit oldest sister, Cynthia, to portray Shabbona's wife, Potanoka, an Indian princess. Cynthia had never been known for her ability to concentrate on small details and was easily distracted during the reading of Albina's letters. As a result, Cynthia had apparently either forgotten or ignored Albina's description of the chief's wife. Although Shabbona was a sizeable man, his girth paled in comparison to that of his wife, Potanoka, who weighed, according to conservative estimates, at least four hundred pounds. Mary Ann and Sarah secretly shared, with uncharitable sisterly glee, the knowledge that Cynthia was completely unaware of the actual appearance of the Indian princess she portrayed.

Albina explained that Shabbona, an Ottawa Indian, was a grand-nephew of Chief Pontiac, had married the daughter of a Pottawatomie chief and upon the death of the old chief, Shabbona took his place as leader of the tribe. Shabbona became allied with the Sauk, Chippewa, and Pottawatomie Indians in a confederation known as "The Three Fires" and became one of their greatest leaders. One of Shabbona's allies at the time was Chief Black Hawk who was a leader of a tribe of Sauk Indians along the Illinois River.

According to Albina, Shabbona had long ago accepted the fact that the white man far outnumbered the Indians and that to survive, he and his people would have to learn to coexist. Shabbona had witnessed the death of his friend Tecumseh after the Battle of Thames in September 1813 where he fought along his side. After this battle, Shabbona had vowed to never again take up arms against the whites. It was a vow that he kept for the remainder of his life.

Albina described Chief Shabbona as a tall, powerful man whose name meant, "strong built like a bear." She also hastened to explain that he was a pleasant, reasonable man who had long been known as a friend of the white man, but that this was not the case with Black Hawk.

Black Hawk had been away from his village in July of 1830 when other leaders of the Sauk and Fox tribes signed a treaty that ceded more than twenty-six million acres of Indian land east of the Mississippi River to the United States Government. When Black Hawk returned and learned of the treaty and that his own village was included in the land sold, he was angry and refused to abandon his land. However, the following year, he and several other chiefs were forced to sign a surrender agreement by which they promised to remain west of the Mississippi River. Black Hawk believed that the white leaders lied and never kept their promises to the Indian and that, therefore, he and his followers were likewise free to ignore the white man's rules.

Determined to regain his land, Black Hawk returned to his village on April 5, 1832. Black Hawk called a war council of his followers and, realizing the high regard in which Shabbona was held, invited him and his warriors to the council. Black Hawk urged the Indians to unite against the white man. Upon learning of Black Hawk's determination to attack the white settlers, Shabbona left the council and went to the cabins of the settlers to warn them of the imminent attack. Chief Shabbona was the hero of the day as he moved quickly to the home of each pioneer settler and prevented their deaths at the hands of Black Hawk and his warriors.

Mary Ann and her siblings bombarded Albina with requests for more stories and were thrilled with each new installment. After exhausting her accounts of Chief Shabbona, Albina moved on to other stories about the Black Hawk War and the responsibility of the army and the Illinois Militia and of dashing young soldiers who had played such an important role. In her letters of 1846 she was happy to describe for her cousins some adventures of a military nature. These were special favorites of Mary Ann's brothers as well as of her uncle Abraham's sons, Ellis, Homer, and William Henry Harrison Montgomery. In these new re-enactments, they enjoyed most playing the role of gallant soldiers. Mary Ann and her sisters were, more often than not, spectators as their brothers and cousins enacted the brave, daring encounters of the soldiers with the Indians.

Although the lives of the settlers had been spared by Shabbona's quick and decisive intervention, Albina had explained that the government quickly alerted the regular army as well as the Illinois Militia to deal with the renegade Indians. Immediately, five brigades of volunteer militia were organized for three months' service. Albina was eager to tell them about the newly elected congressman from Illinois, Abraham Lincoln, who had been one of those soldiers.

On April 7, 1832, twenty-three-year-old Abraham Lincoln was elected captain of his company in the Thirty-first Illinois Volunteer Militia. Lincoln's company of seventy men had been organized in Sangamon County. From there they were ordered to the south bank of Rock River to the frontier post of Dixon's Ferry. In addition to the ferry, operator John Dixon and his family ran a tavern located along a trail that ran from Galena to the ferry then eastward through the counties of DeKalb, Kane,

*Captain Abraham Lincoln*
*31st Illinois Volunteer Militia*
*1832 Black Hawk War*
COURTESY OF NORTHERN ILLINOIS UNIVERSITY

*Lt. Jefferson Davis*
*First U.S. Infantry*
*1832 Black Hawk War*
COURTESY OF NORTHERN ILLINOIS UNIVERSITY

DuPage, and Cook to Chicago. The tavern was a ninety-foot rambling log structure that provided food and lodging to travelers. It was at this frontier post that regular army forces sent to the area met men and officers of the newly formed Illinois Militia. Once assembled there, officers of the regular army invited officers of the militia to join them at meals to further the cause of camaraderie. And so it was that militia captain Abraham Lincoln sat down to dinner with twenty-four-year-old West Point graduate, Lieutenant Jefferson Finis Davis of the First U.S. Infantry in 1832. Neither the young boys who so enjoyed impersonating these young officers, nor the two men, could have guessed what destiny lay before them all.

*Dixon's Ferry*
*Site of meeting place of Lincoln and Davis, 1832.*
COURTESY OF NORTHERN ILLINOIS UNIVERSITY

Lincoln served until July 10, however, although his unit did a considerable amount of marching throughout northern Illinois, he was not involved in combat, while Lieutenant Davis and the regular army were actively involved in the fighting and in the capture of Black Hawk. In many cases those units who faced Black Hawk and his forces in battle, were determined to not only force the Indians out, but were also bent on annihilating them.

The attack by the militia was brutal and merciless, as all of Black Hawk's tribe were either slaughtered or captured. In her first letters about the soldiers' encounters with Black Hawk's men, Albina provided no real details. However, as with most young boys playing at war, the more bloody and violent the struggle, the more entertaining they found it. The boys constantly pressed Albina for more specifics, and the more gruesome the details, the better they liked it. These young boys in southern Ohio never expected that they would one day find themselves propelled into a war of far greater bloodshed and duration than the one they reenacted in their youth.

## Chief Shabbona, a Welcome Guest and Valued Friend

The other members of the Montgomery family who had settled in Bureau County enjoyed Albina's stories about entertaining Chief Shabbona as much their family in Ohio. It was not long before they too had the opportunity to entertain the old chief. Chief Shabbona and his wife were always eager to visit their friends among the whites and to share the bounty of their host's dinner table. In particular, they enjoyed the freshly baked bread prepared by the pioneers and always expected their host family to offer whatever leftovers there might be to take home. Shabbona and his wife were intrigued by the methods used by white settlers to prepare meat and would often bring with them some offering from their hunt. The Montgomery family was grateful for the venison, wild turkeys, geese and other meat they brought and were more than happy to prepare the meal, which always included gravy, made from the drippings from the meat. It was a delectable dish, which Shabbona and his wife consumed with great gusto. It was clear to all who knew them that beauty is in the eye of the beholder and that Shabbona and Potanoka were as devoted to each other as they were to a hearty meal.

## Francina Montgomery

The widow Charlotte Montgomery and her sister-in-law Nancy Montgomery wrote to each other whenever some event of importance occurred within their respective families. Mary Ann and her siblings were always excited by the arrival of any letters from Illinois and eagerly waited for their mother, Nancy, to share the news with them. Charlotte conceded that both she and her children were adjusting better than expected to

*Elijah and Francina Montgomery McNitt*

prairie life and that young Francina was being courted by nineteen-year-old New York native, Elijah McNitt. A few months later, Aunt Charlotte was happy to share the news that Francina and Elijah were married on New Year's Day 1845 in Rock Falls, Whiteside County, Illinois. She had hoped that her daughter and new son-in-law might travel to Ohio for a visit and to sell Francina's share of her father's estate, but was disappointed that they had decided instead to hire an attorney to handle the paperwork on Francina's behalf. Charlotte was happy to report however, that the couple had moved to Bureau County and were neighbors of the rest of the Montgomery clan

Mary Ann and her sisters wanted to know more about cousin Francina's new husband. Aunt Charlotte's letters, while welcome, were never as lengthy or full of detail as cousin Albina's and the girls urged their mother to write to Albina with their questions. As usual,

Albina was only too happy to comply. She explained that early in his young life in New York, Elijah had been exposed to and influenced by the temperance movement. Elijah was especially swayed by the fiery sermons of Methodist preachers who urged parishioners to avoid the use of "demon rum." They warned of the moral decay and eternal damnation that would be the inevitable fate of all the poor sinners who failed to heed their warnings. Elijah pointed out that it was not just the churches that had influenced him, but also the New York newspapers that insisted that the social and moral problems of the nation were the direct result of abuse of liquor by the population. Albina noted that those early experiences clearly made an impact on the young Elijah, and that he was devoted to the cause. She praised him for being a devout Christian, but also pointed out that he was a stern man of iron principles. Elijah welcomed every opportunity to inform others of the evils of whisky and spirits and to convince them of the importance of abstinence. Albina also confided that Elijah was fortunate that Francina was such a docile and obedient wife who was willing to embrace her husband's views. A few years after their marriage, Elijah decided that the best way to promote his strong convictions was to open his home as a hotel or inn, one which, of course, did not serve spirits. He could charge a small fee for lodging and food, promote his favorite cause, and still be able to manage his small farm. Albina was quick to point out to her Ohio cousins that the greater portion of work involved in this new venture, i.e., the additional cleaning, cooking, and laundry while caring for young children, fell to Francina. Throughout most of their married life, Francina and Elijah and their twelve children continued to welcome their paying guests into the alcohol-free hospitality of their home.

## The Widow, Aunt Charlotte

In the autumn of 1846, Charlotte was experiencing a period of apparent remission of her illness and had begun to enjoy her new life on the prairie. She had even received a proposal of marriage and wrote to Nancy to share the news of the upcoming event. On October 22, at

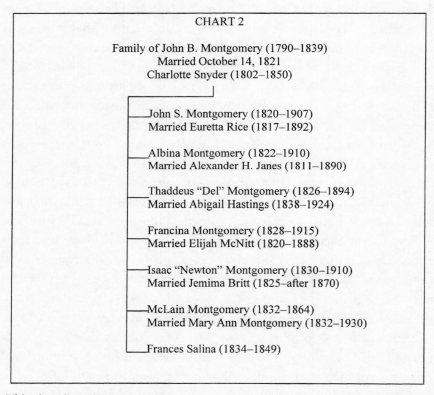

CHART 2

Family of John B. Montgomery (1790–1839)
Married October 14, 1821
Charlotte Snyder (1802–1850)

John S. Montgomery (1820–1907)
Married Euretta Rice (1817–1892)

Albina Montgomery (1822–1910)
Married Alexander H. Janes (1811–1890)

Thaddeus "Del" Montgomery (1826–1894)
Married Abigail Hastings (1838–1924)

Francina Montgomery (1828–1915)
Married Elijah McNitt (1820–1888)

Isaac "Newton" Montgomery (1830–1910)
Married Jemima Britt (1825–after 1870)

McLain Montgomery (1832–1864)
Married Mary Ann Montgomery (1832–1930)

Frances Salina (1834–1849)

This chart lists all of the known children of John B. Montgomery and Charlotte
Snyder with the exception of son William J. who died as an infant in 1824.

age forty-four, Charlotte married John Leonard in Bureau County. Her letter was full of excitement and she felt confident that her new husband would bring happiness and security to her life. She even began to enumerate the blessings she was enjoying. She was still young and was proud of the three young grandchildren who provided such joy to the household of her daughter Albina. She looked forward to spending her old age in the company of her children and even more grandchildren. Only two of her children, McLain and Frances Salina, were still at home and she was happy and optimistic.

When Nancy finally received another letter from Illinois in 1847, it came from Charlotte's oldest daughter, twenty-four-year-old Albina, who shared the sad news that her mother's condition was suddenly much worse than before. She was pale, had lost considerable weight and although the laudanum seemed to give her some relief, Albina feared that her mother had become so dependent upon the drug that she could not survive without it. The disease was progressing rapidly and her mother's spirit seemed crushed and she appeared to be slipping deeper and deeper into depression and was reluctant to talk to family. Albina's letter of 1849 contained even more distressing news. John Leonard had abandoned his ailing wife and stepchildren never to return.

After her husband's departure, her sixteen-year-old son, McLain, and fourteen-year-old daughter, Salina, were forced to find employment outside the home.

## Salina Montgomery and the Banditti of the Prairie

Albina kept her Ohio cousins informed as best she could regarding her mother's condition and the welfare of her two younger siblings. Albina and her husband offered McLain a job on their nearby farm. She mentioned that her younger brother didn't find it to be a particularly exciting job, but pointed out that it offered reliable and safe employment. Albina wasn't quite so sure about fourteen-year-old Salina. Albina acknowledged that her young sister was a lot like she had been at that age. In other words, Salina was a little headstrong and eager for some excitement in her life. Albina had, after all, been the first to leave the family and come to Illinois. But Albina confided that she had an uneasy feeling when Salina left home for her new job as a maid in a local tavern run by Charles Croft. Albina mentioned that there had long been whispered rumors about the questionable character of Croft and his friends, but she did not provide any details about those rumors. She ended her letter with the conclusion that she probably worried too much and that the money from Salina's job would be helpful to her ailing mother. It would be several months before the Montgomery family in Ohio would hear from Illinois again, and none of the news would be good.

Charles Croft and his wife, Mary Ann, owned and operated a tavern as well as the tollhouse on the Cleveland Turnpike in Lee County, East Grove Township, which adjoined Bureau County to the north. Croft had long been viewed with suspicion by many of his neighbors and was believed to be a member of a group of petty thieves and cutthroats known as the "Banditti of the Prairie."

During the mid-nineteenth century there were numerous such bands in the Midwest in Indiana, Illinois, Missouri, and Iowa. The majority, however, were located in the northern Illinois counties of Lee, DeKalb, Ogle, and Winnebago. The banditti were so entrenched within many communities that they held public office and often served on juries that refused to convict one of their own. An even bigger problem was the fear that these bands inflicted upon their victims through intimidation and violence. The problem became so severe that Ogle and Winnebago counties organized volunteer vigilante groups to resolve an issue which local law enforcement seemed incapable of handling. These groups, known as "regulators," tracked down and meted out their own form of justice swiftly and efficiently.

Notoriety of these lawless banditti extended nationwide with the publication of Edward Bonney's personal tale of his encounter with a group of such thugs in Iowa who were responsible for the torture and murder of George Davenport, a well-known and respected pioneer. Bonney was a self-styled private detective and bounty hunter who infiltrated the banditti by assuming the role of a counterfeiter. Bonney identified the murderers of Davenport and, as a result, three of the four men were hanged. Afterwards, Bonney, himself, was indicted for murder, but was later acquitted. Bonney's book, *Banditti of the Prairie, or The Murderer's Doom* was published by Homeward Publications, Chicago, Illinois, in 1850. It sold for seventy-five cents per copy and was an instant best seller.

In northern Illinois these bands of thugs had nearly been eradicated from several counties by the actions of local regulators. In Ogle County, regulators had captured, held their own trials and hanged several of the leaders, thus restoring a semblance of law and order. In neighboring Lee County, however, the banditti were at the height of their activities from 1843 to 1850.

The crimes most often attributed to Croft included counterfeiting, horse stealing, and, finally, the worst accusation of all being that he was responsible for the robbery and murder of a peddler who had disappeared after stopping at the tavern.

According to her family, Salina had returned to her mother's home in late July, shortly after the disappearance of the peddler, and confided that she did not want to return to work because she feared for her life. When questioned about her fears, she revealed that she had witnessed the murder of the peddler and that Croft had warned her that he would kill her if she ever told anyone. On Wednesday, August 1, 1849, Salina was finally persuaded to return to work. She was never to be seen alive again.

The circumstances of her death and of the deaths of her accused killers were, and are, the source of much speculation even today. Published accounts were based upon the reports given by the men in the search party. Those men were friends and neighbors of the Montgomery family and, painful as it was, kept the family informed of their progress. Chief among those directly involved in the search were Hira Axtell, William Andrus, Samuel Meek, and his son, Richard Meek, Moses Curtis, Patrick McFadden, and Constable Joseph Willard, all of whom were neighbors in Hamilton Township, Lee County. It appears that Lee County, Illinois, may have had its own regulators.

The first to be alerted to Salina's disappearance was fifty-nine-year-old Hira Axtell, a native of New York. On August 2, Hira was paid a visit by Croft who asked if he knew where young Salina might be. Croft expressed concern that the girl had left and had taken all of her clothes with her. Croft further stated that the girl's family had no idea where she had gone and were concerned.

There was something about Croft's demeanor, coupled with his shady reputation that caused Hira to be suspicious. After Croft departed, Hira went to his neighbor, William Andrus and the two decided to begin a search for the young girl. They went to the tavern operated by Croft where they reportedly found four men in the company of Croft. They did not recognize two of the men; however, the other two, Samuel Perkins and Eli Shaw, were well known to Hira and William. Both Perkins and Shaw were suspected members of the notorious banditti.

Perkins was a colorful character whom the locals referred to as Sam Patch. He was easily recognized by his attire, which consisted of tattered clothes, moccasins, and a straw hat. According to Axtell and Andrus, they were immediately suspicious of Croft and his associates, but decided that the first order of business was to find the young girl. They proceeded to organize a posse of local men and began to search for Salina.

The posse searched throughout the remainder of the day and continued through the night until noon of the following day. On Friday, August 3, the posse returned to Croft's establishment and searched the girl's room on the second floor of the tavern. The searchers reported that they had found, under a floorboard, the girl's clothing as well as tools for counterfeiting half dollars.

The next event reported by the men of the search party added greatly to the eerie and ominous nature of the investigation. According to sixty-seven-year-old Pennsylvania native Samuel Meek, he and his neighbor, thirty-six year-old Irishman Patrick McFadden decided to visit a local fortuneteller. According to Meek and McFadden, the fortuneteller was known to have exceptional psychic powers and revealed to them that five men had murdered young Salina and that the murderer wore neither boots nor was barefooted, was dressed in rags and wore a straw hat. Meek and McFadden also claimed that the old fortuneteller prophesied that none of the five would ever be convicted of murder.

Word of the fortuneteller's prediction spread quickly among the men in the search party and sixty-one-year-old, Massachusetts native James Blair, of Amboy Township, returned home for dinner to share the story with his wife. Blair's wife, Fanny, excitedly told him some news of her own. Earlier that day, Sam Patch Perkins had appeared at her door, and according to Fanny, looked very sick, and asked about the progress of the search party. Perkins had also inquired whether or not the posse had searched the lower bayou. Blair quickly returned to the searchers and shared this information. It was discovered that earlier in the day, Perkins and his wife, Sarah, had moved from their shanty which sat halfway between the Croft tavern and the bayou, to the home of his father-in-law, Reuben Bridgeman, in Amboy Township.

Constable Joseph Williard and his deputy, Richard Meek, were notified and a warrant was issued for Perkins's arrest. They immediately went to Bridgeman's home in search of the suspect. Bridgeman told them that his son-in-law had left about four o'clock in the afternoon to hunt prairie chickens in the cornfield, but had not yet returned. According to Williard and Meek, the old man also confided that he had heard a shot later on near the old cottonwood tree, but had not gone to investigate.

The posse was again assembled and about ten o'clock that night, under a full moon, they found the dead body of Sam Perkins lying on his back, under an old cottonwood tree. Witnesses to the scene all gave identical descriptions. They reported that Perkins was still holding his rifle and the toe of one foot, encased in a moccasin, was thrust through the trigger guard of the rifle. A coroner's inquest was held immediately and the resulting opinion was that Perkins had committed suicide by shooting himself in the head.

The next day, the posse searched the bayou and found the body of young Salina Montgomery in the swamp area around Inlet Creek with severe bruising about her face. The sheriff's conclusion was that she had been hit by a heavy object, but others insisted that there was a bullet hole in her forehead.

By this time, word of Salina's death had reached nearly every home for miles around, and many had joined in the search for the girl. The Lee County coroner, Parker, immediately impaneled a jury to conduct an inquest. On August 4, witnesses were sworn and gave their testimony and the jury rendered the verdict that young Salina Montgomery came to her death by violence and that one Sam Perkins, late of Lee County, was the was the man who had caused her death.

Warrants were issued for Croft and for Eli Shaw. Later that day, Shaw's dead body was discovered near the Meek home in a wagon with a half-empty bottle of whisky nearby. The whisky had apparently been laced with strychnine. For some unknown reason, the coroner did not immediately hold an inquest regarding Shaw's death. In fact, it was not until March of the following year that an inquest was finally held. The jury concluded that there was not sufficient evidence to determine the cause of Shaw's death.

Hira Axtell, Moses Curtis[s], and W. B. Stuart were deputized to arrest Charle Croft. When they arrived at the tavern, there was clear evidence that Croft was about to take flight. There was a horse hitched to a wagon that was loaded with a large trunk. When they peered through the window, they saw Croft collecting his weapons and loading a pistol. The three men burst through the door and over powered the surprised Croft and took him to Dixon, the county seat, to jail.

Croft was indicted on August 23, 1849, and was confined in the Dixon jail, purportedly awaiting a trial. However, no trial date was set and on the afternoon of November 22, 1849, the jailer reported that he had found his prisoner dead. Croft's throat had been cut with a razor. Upon contemplating the day's events, the jailer recalled that Mary Ann Croft had been permitted to visit her husband earlier in the day and had brought with her a loaf of freshly baked bread. Apparently, folks concluded, there must have been a razor baked into the loaf. The following day, November 23, a coroner's inquest was held and the jury issued their verdict that Croft had died at his own hands by cutting his own throat. For the good people of Lee County, this was a satisfactory ending to the most regrettable murder of young Salina Montgomery. The final note to the story is that with the death of Charles Croft in November of 1849, the reign of terror caused by the thugs and cutthroats known as the banditti of the prairie had ended forever in Lee County.

The series of events that resulted in Salina's death and the pursuit of her killers was overwhelming to the family and apparently were too painful to describe in writing. It was not until 1850 that Mary Ann and her family received the sad news that her young cousin Salina had been murdered. It seemed impossible that such a thing could have happened to one so young and that men like the banditti had been allowed to exert so much violence on the innocent. In that same letter they learned of Charlotte's failed battle with tuberculosis. They felt certain that the horrid death of young Salina had hastened her mother's death.

## John Stanley Montgomery

The eldest of the Montgomery siblings, John S. Montgomery, married the widow, Euretta A. Bell on August 17, 1848, in Bureau County and settled on a prairie farm. John was the least adventurous of the Illinois Montgomery's and contented himself with the duties of a farmer and enjoyed the companionship of his wife and four children and ten grandchildren. He was a man of simple pleasures. Although he lived a

*John Stanley Montgomery*

long and productive life as a well-respected member of his community, one of his simple pleasures ultimately proved to be fatal to him. He, like many members of the family, both male and female, loved to smoke a pipe. On June 14, 1907, John died from cancer of the lip.

## Isaac Newton Montgomery

Newton, as he was known to family, was just five foot five, and thus, the shortest of the Montgomery men. He had pale blue eyes and a pale complexion and was not a particularly hardy individual and his family often noted that he suffered from a variety of illnesses, which often left him incapacited for long periods of time. It appeared that Newton was destined to face a life of hardship and adversity. On May 9, 1854, twenty-four-year-old Newton married thirty-year-old widow, Jemima Ann Britt, a native of Virginia whose husband, Joseph Robinson, had died the preceding year. Newton, who owned no land of his own and worked as a farm laborer, found himself with responsibility for a wife and five stepchildren, with the youngest being just one year old. The family was concerned that circumstances did not bode well for the marriage.

## Thaddeus Delorain Montgomery

The tallest of the Montgomery clan at six feet in height with dark eyes and hair, was Thaddeus Delorain Montgomery, whom everyone called "Del." Like all the Montgomery men he was a skilled hunter, but for Del it was more than an occasional activity. He had specifically selected his home near one of the swampy areas where he expected to take advantage of the many fur-bearing animals that had been such an important part of the early economy of the area. Unfortunately for Del, the once high demand from Europe for beaver pelts had dwindled as had the beaver population itself. By the early 1840s many of the wild species once so prevalent in the area had been over exploited. Del was, however, determined to prove his skills and reluctant to concede to the life of a farmer. The result was a heavy reliance on the trapping of muskrats, foxes, and mink, which were also in short supply. In order to be successful in this endeavor, it was often necessary to travel. It was not unusual for Del to be away from home for weeks in the winter often traveling north to Wisconsin to hunt and trap there.

On May 24, 1858, thirty-two-year-old Del married Abigail, the vivacious twenty-year-old daughter of Oliver Hazard Hastings. Abigail was an energetic and dutiful wife who apparently did not object to her husband's many absences as he tended to his traps, and like many of the women of the day, enjoyed smoking her pipe as much as any man.

## McLain Montgomery

McLain had been a dutiful son who had helped to care for his ailing mother. Upon her death and the murder of his sister, Salina, the eighteen-year-old felt alone and forsaken. Both his father and mother were gone and his older siblings, Albina, Francina, and John were married with families of their own. Brother Del was consumed with his hunting and trapping and Newton, well, Newton seemed as lost as he. His emotional response to this profound sense of loneliness was one of unrestrained abandon. Life was too short not to be enjoyed and he threw himself into a variety of reckless behaviors which his siblings found troubling. This was especially true of his brother-in-law Elijah McNitt, who was determined to reform the young man's behavior. But for a while, at least, McLain was determined to experience as much of life as he could.

## Exciting Events in Ottawa

The Montgomery family was excited to attend any function that provided an entertaining break from their daily routine. They attended one such event on the Fourth of July, 1857, at a local fair in Ottawa, LaSalle County, which neighbors Bureau County. And this Fourth of July celebration promised to be especially exciting as Chief Shabbona and his wife were expected to attend. Chief Shabbona's friendship to the white settlers of the area was recognized and rewarded by all who knew him and he was often present at public events as an honored guest.

The evening's activities included a grand ball. At this event, the young ladies, dressed in their finest gowns, participated in a competition to determine which of them excelled in grace and beauty. Albina and her husband, like their neighbors, beamed with pride as their oldest daughters were introduced. Each of the families was certain that their daughter would surely be selected as the most beautiful. Chief Shabbona was invited to judge the event, and viewed each of the young women in a solemn and critical manner as they passed by. When called upon to proclaim a winner, ever the prudent and diplomatic gentleman, he turned to his wife and patted her upon her most abundant frame and said, "Much, heap, big, prettiest squaw." His remark brought approving smiles and applause from all in attendance, with the exception of the young ladies of the contest.

The following year, on August 21, 1858, several members of the Montgomery family joined the more than twelve thousand people who traveled in sweltering heat to nearby Ottawa to listen to a debate between Abraham Lincoln and Stephen A. Douglas. *The Chicago Press and Tribune,* August 25, 1858, reported that by eight o'clock in the morning the streets and avenues leading into town "were so enveloped with dust that the town resembled a vast smoke house" with large processions of people pouring in from every direction "like an army with banners."

This was the first of seven debates in the campaign for the U.S. Senate seat from Illinois. News coverage for the event was extensive and reporters from all over the state were there and depending upon the political affiliation of each paper, presented a partisan account of the event. Democrat papers supporting Douglas were convinced that his arguments had been the most persuasive, while Republican papers were equally convinced that Lincoln had verbally destroyed the "Little Giant." Owen Lovejoy, a former preacher at the Congregationalist Church at Princeton, Bureau County, a renowned orator and recently elected member of Congress, was there to promote Lincoln and to speak in support of the antislavery movement.

Also present among the honored guests that day was Chief Shabbona who was invited to share the platform with the other dignitaries. Those sitting near the old chief reported that Shabbona showed emotion only once during the debate. He was visibly angered when Stephen A. Douglas proclaimed his opposition to "citizenship for Negroes, Indians, and other inferior races."

This was one of the last public functions attended by the old chief, who died July 22, 1859, at eighty-four years of age. He knew that Lincoln had lost his bid for the U.S. Senate but did not live to witness the election of his old friend to the presidency in 1860.

*Chief Shabbona*
*Photo taken the year he died, 1859.*
COURTESY OF NORTHERN ILLINOIS UNIVERSITY

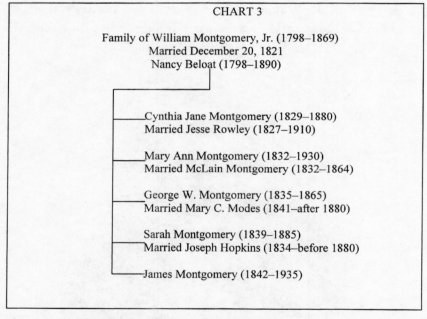

CHART 3

Family of William Montgomery, Jr. (1798–1869)
Married December 20, 1821
Nancy Beloat (1798–1890)

Cynthia Jane Montgomery (1829–1880)
Married Jesse Rowley (1827–1910)

Mary Ann Montgomery (1832–1930)
Married McLain Montgomery (1832–1864)

George W. Montgomery (1835–1865)
Married Mary C. Modes (1841–after 1880)

Sarah Montgomery (1839–1885)
Married Joseph Hopkins (1834–before 1880)

James Montgomery (1842–1935)

This chart lists all of the known children of William Montgomery, Jr., and Nancy Beloat.

# CHAPTER 3

# A Reunion in Ohio

## Family Routine in Southern Ohio

After the mysterious disappearance of John B. Montgomery, and the eventual departure of his widow and children to Illinois, William Montgomery, Jr., and his wife Nancy faced the routine activities common to farm families. For William, things would never be the same after the exodus of so many family members. His own trips down the Mississippi to New Orleans to take crops to market became more frequent and of longer duration and Nancy feared that, some day he too, like his brother John, might not return.

Despite her concerns, she found consolation in the events of her children's lives. She was pleased when eldest daughter, Cynthia, upon her marriage to Jesse Rowley in 1849, settled near the family homestead on Dogwood Ridge. Daughter Sarah and husband Joseph Hopkins, who worked at the mills, lived in nearby Harrison Township and visited often, and daughter Mary Ann and sons George W. and James were still at home to help with the farm chores. Notwithstanding his frequent absences, her husband had insisted that his children have a good education and had instilled in them his appreciation for literature and music. Nancy, like other women in similar situations, chose to embrace her blessings and to make the best of whatever challenges life might present.

## McLain Montgomery's Trip Home

On November 30, 1853, McLain Montgomery celebrated his twenty-first birthday. The following day, Thursday, December 1, he began his journey to Ohio to sell his share of inherited land. It was a timely visit that would allow him to spend the Christmas holidays with his aunt Nancy and uncle William Montgomery on Dogwood Ridge.

McLain's cousin, Mary Ann was thoroughly charmed

*McLain Montgomery*

by the stories he told about the excitement of life on the prairie. It seemed to her that, clearly, the life enjoyed by her Illinois cousins was far more interesting than hers in southern Ohio. For McLain, the visit prompted fond memories of his earlier years at the old homestead and the festivities of the holiday season only intensified his feelings for the place. It was with regret that he left his friends and family in Scioto County in mid January to return to Illinois with money in his pocket from the sale of the land. The good thing was, that he now had funds with which to purchase a place of his own.

Upon his return to Illinois he wrote the first of many letters to family members in Ohio. His cousin Mary Ann saved and treasured each piece of correspondence from McLain and began her collection of the letters that would become such an anchor in her world.

January 22, 1853

To Nancy Montgomery.

Dear Aunt, after a quick and pleasant journey, I arrived here on Wednesday last and found the folks all well and doing well. I am now at Mr. Janes's and I find it is colder weather than I have seen before. This winter I froze my ears last Friday crossing the prairie and I think that it is colder than you ever seen it in Ohio. But I have told you enough about the cold weather. Delorain is at LaSalle and Newton is at East Grove. John is at home setting in the corner holding the Baby. Albina is setting by the stove and smoking and she says that she wishes you was here too so that you could smoke with her, but as you are not, she sends you a piece of her dress for you to remember her by. She says she would be glad to see you all. Francina is at Dover. All of her folks is well and she sends her best respects to you all. I have no more news that is worth writing. I am well and I hope that the same blessing rests with you all. You have my best wishes through life.

Your affectionate nephew. McLain Montgomery

To Nancy Montgomery

The letter also contained the following brief message to his cousin George, along with a rather cryptic message to be passed along to Mary Ann. The motivation for this cautionary advice is unknown.

To George Mont.

Dear Cousin. I have not meant to write this time, but in hope that I can find more to write next time. I want you to write to me as soon as you get this. Direct your letter to Lasalle Co. and Lasalle Post office. I cannot find any more news and it is getting dark and I am most froze.

One word to you and Mary both and that is the best way to cure a burn is to keep your fingers out of the fire so the best way to keep out of a bad scrape is be safe and then you will never [be] troubled to get out. If you can read this you can do more than I can. I write it in the dark and it will take two Portsmouth lawyers to read it for you. I want you to write all the news and more to.

McLain M. to George Montgomery

P.S. remember the post office Lasalle, Laxalle Co. Ill. Give my love to all who may enquire. Good by.

LaSalle P.O., Lasalle County.

One month later, McLain's older brother, Newton Montgomery also wrote to his Scioto County relatives. As usual, Newton was feeling poorly.

> February 8, 1854
> East Grove, Lee County, Illinois
>
> My Dear cousin,
>
> I take my pen in hand to inform [you] how my health is. I have not seen a well day since I left Ohio and for that curse I have written before. It is very cold here today and I have to stay in the house all the time. The snow is on the ground and the wind blows. Tell Mary that I would be very glad to see her. Give my respects to George and James. Tell Aunt to write to me soon. Direct your letter to Dover, Bureau, Co., Ill. You must excuse this short awkward letter for I must go to bed.
>
> Forget me not
> Forget me never
> Till the son [*sic*] is set forever.
> Your affectionate Cousin
> I.N. Montgomery
> To Sarah Montgomery
> So Good By

As the weather improved and spring burst forth on the northern prairie, Newton also enjoyed better health and a renewed interest in life, and married the widow Robinson. This was perhaps not the wisest of decisions since Newton had few economic prospects, owned no land of his own and worked as a farm laborer for family and friends.

In August of 1854 McLain continued his correspondence to his aunt Nancy and revealed that he had, for some time been writing to cousin George. His letter seems to suggest that he considered himself a reformed man and that he had abandoned the ways of his youth and now, no doubt influenced by his sister Francina and her husband, Elijah, embraced the cause of temperance.

> August 25th 1854
> Dover, Bureau Co. Ill.

Respected Aunt,

I sit down to write a few lines to you. My writing has, heretofore been confined to George for the reason that I have not had time to write much. Besides, I have to write to the girls once in a while to keep them in a good humor. I am now at Dover full of life and hope. I enjoy health with all its blessings surrounded with friends. I have nothing to wish for to make me happy but to know that those I love and esteem are enjoying the same God's blessings. Changeable in deed are the scenes I have prayed through since I left the old farm on Dogwood Ridge. I have sometimes almost resolved to come back and spend the winter in the neighborhood of Wheelersburg. But I cannot do it often. So I think of the happy hours I passed during the long evenings of December. Although I am happy here I sometimes wish I could be there and enjoy company of you and your family.

I am not as well now as I was then. I have become a sober thinking man, in truth I am what the young folks call the old man. I am a stranger to the ballroom and likewise to the grocery. I am a true friend to the cause of temperance and I do all in my power to promote its rise and progress.

I am now at work for Elijah McNitt, my brother-in-law. He keeps a temperance house here in Dover. I am working now to pay for a town lot which I have bought. Francine is not very well but she is able to be at work & Albina was well the last time I heard from her. John is well and is old enough to have two son-in-laws and one grandchild. Delorain was well the last time of heard from him. Newton is well, but his wife is not.

I have told you about all the folks. Now I will tell you about the country at the time I write. I am setting at a window which looks out on a Prairie about 15 miles long and 12 wide. A cool breeze comes in at the window where I set and makes my place a pleasant one to [see] the quiet little town of Dover to good advantage with its shady walks and then there is something so still and peaceful hanging over the place that makes me love it. I wish you was here. I am sure you would enjoy the scenery the wide extending Prairies stretching so far as the eye can reach. Dotted over with farms but it is very dry and warm. We have not had any rain for a long time and the corn and potatoes are suffering for something to drink and there is no prospects for rain yet. Fruit is scarce here on account of the late frosts in the spring. I want you to eat one good peach for me. As for apples, I can get enough to eat, but none to spare.

The final portion of the letter is an appeal for correspondence from his Ohio cousins and for news about Uncle William, who was once again on a trip of unknown duration, down the Mississippi to take goods to market.

> Tell Mary I have not yet forgotten her and I want her to write a letter to me. And Sarah, I want she should write. Tell George the longest letter he can write will not a bit too long for me to read and Cyntha must not be forgot. I want to hear from her. Tell James I would like to be there this fall and help drive the Majors corn off south. But if I don't quit writing you will get tired of reading and I am tired of writing. If you get any news from Uncle William, I want you to tell me how [he] is getting along and when he is coming home. Give my love to all, but be sure and keep a good share for yourself. Write soon.

> McLain Montgomery to his Aunt Nancy Montgomery.
> Direct to Dover, Bureau Co. Ill.

The following to cousin George is the last of the prewar letters written by McLain to his Ohio relatives. Although he proclaimed his intention to remain a bachelor forever, events over the next few years reveal the fallacy of his prophecy. It appears that he had tired of life on the prairie and had opted to see a little more of the world and was bound for the more cosmopolitan life of Baton Rouge, Louisiana.

> Peru [LaSalle County, Illinois]
> March 5th 1856

> Dear cousin. It is a long time since I heard from you and I expect you have quite forgot me, but I intend to wake up your memory. I wrote to you almost a year ago and have never heard from you since. Maybe you thought my letter was not worth an answer. Perhaps it was not. I don't know; however, I thought I would not write again until I heard form you. But as I am going to change my position and I thought I would let you know where to write if the notion should take you. I expect to go south as soon as the ice floats out which will not be long. But the news of the day, don't be surprised when I tell you I am single yet and expect to remain so till the last trump[et] shall sound. Yes, I will remain single til old Bruner shall stand on Tick Ridge and say that time shall be no

more, as the old preacher says when the judgment gun snaps twice.

We have had a very cold winter here. The ice on the river is 3 feet thick and the snow is from one to 5 feet deep. We have not had any rain here for six months to do any good. Dell is in Wisconsin. Newton is out to Walnut Grove. His house smokes very bad and strange to say it smokes worst when the fire is out. Happy is the man who has no wife at all. He can live at his ease and keep Bachelors hall. All of the rest are well now.

George, I tell you what it is if you don't answer this letter. I will cross you off of my book. I want you to write all the news. Tell the girls if they are not married to come here in haste, if they want to secure a good bargain. Here is men of every size, shape and age, all in search of a wife.

Now George before you open this letter, just take down your old fiddle and play "Jack Monroe" for me. I can play the fiddle some myself. Can play well, God, I swear I can play "Cape On The Green" most as well as George can, but I have sold my fiddle and I want you to play "Jack M." But it is no use of my telling you again.

The following inquiries concern the health of some of the Montgomery friends in Porter Township. Seventy-nine-year-old George B. Powell, a native of Connecticut, was a wealthy farmer who owned nearly 250 acres of Porter Township real estate. The other people mentioned have not been identified. Tick Ridge, like Dogwood Ridge is located in Wheelersburg.

Tell me now is old Powell alive yet. Has the old major got his corn gathered yet. Is Andy and Albina live yet. Have they got any tobacco? Has Henry shot himself lately? Has any of you been out there to get your guts stuffed? In short, I want you to tell me all about Tick Ridge and the people in general. Tell Aunt I have not forgot her yet. Before you open this write to me and direct your letter to Baton Rouge. Farewell George. Give my love to Aunt and the girls. Keep a share for yourself and James. Tell him to take care of the days of his youth and live in hopes of seeing me again. Good By.

To George Montgomery
McLain Montgomery
Write soon. Direct to Baton Rouge, LA.

Don't Forget

As for southern Ohio, the economy was still booming and by 1850 it ranked second in the United States in the production of iron and the Hanging Rock region became one of Ohio's first industrial areas. The boom continued and on July 10, 1860, the census revealed that the town of Wheelersburg had grown to a population of 1,880. Enumerated within that number was twenty-eight-year-old McLain Montgomery who was dwelling within the household of his aunt Nancy and uncle William Montgomery. On November 29, 1860, McLain and his cousin Mary Ann Montgomery were married in Scioto County, Ohio.

**CHAPTER 4**

# The War Begins

## Response to the President's Call to Arms

Southern Ohio's economy remained strong and in 1861, Ohio was ranked fourth among all states in industrial activity. The state enjoyed continued economic success throughout the Civil War as it produced armaments, including the iron plate used on the Union's ironclad *Monitor*. Ohio prided itself on having more miles of railroad tracks than any other state and the time period was known as Ohio's Iron Age. Scioto County, alone, had a total of ten blast furnaces operating, and many men who worked in them were soon called to arms. Although the area enjoyed great prosperity from the furnaces, the boom would eventually come to an end in the 1870s. This was due largely to over exploitation of the resources of the area. But, while it lasted, the area enjoyed the prosperity of its wartime endeavors.

In addition to the huge economic and social changes resulting from the Civil War, it also brought some bitter political disputes to the area. Ohio's southern border that was delineated by the Ohio River stretched 436 miles, which touched the slaveholding states of western Virginia and Kentucky. Some members of the Montgomery family, like many people in southern Ohio, traced their own roots to these two states and the mere idea of taking up arms against family and neighbors was abhorrent to them. Although the Montgomerys had come to Ohio from Pennsylvania, both John B. and William Montgomery, Jr., had married women who had been born in Virginia. Neither they nor their family could understand why their political leaders seemed either unable or unwilling to resolve the issue through compromise and diplomacy. Even as one by one southern states seceded from the Union, they steadfastly rejected the idea that their sons might be forced into armed conflict against their southern kin.

The situation changed dramatically, however, when the family and their neighbors learned of the attack on Fort Sumter. Despite their former objections, the folks of southern Ohio felt first disbelief followed by anger and then a surge of patriotic conscience. The April 12, 1861, actions of Confederate brigadier general P. G. T. Beauregard could not be ignored. He had fired upon fellow Americans when Maj. Robert Anderson had refused to surrender the Union garrison in Charleston Harbor to Confederate forces. Three days later, President Lincoln issued the first of many calls for Union volunteers, and mothers, wives, sisters, and children understood that their own objections to war would fall upon deaf ears. As the war progressed and President Lincoln was forced to call for an ever-increasing number of troops, Montgomery men, like their friends and neighbors, answered the call.

Over the course of the war more than 320,000 Ohio men and more than 250,000 Illinois men served in the Union army. In fact, the war and their shared experiences clearly drew the two branches of the Montgomery family closer together. Although they served in different regiments and from different states, the descendants of William Montgomery all served in the western theater of the war. Female descendants waited fearfully as their husbands, brothers and cousins left home and family to fulfill their obligations. On occasion, these men found themselves stationed near to each other and thus, had an opportunity to visit and share information about family and friends as

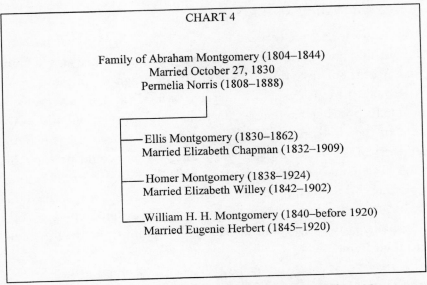

CHART 4

Family of Abraham Montgomery (1804–1844)
Married October 27, 1830
Permelia Norris (1808–1888)

—— Ellis Montgomery (1830–1862)
Married Elizabeth Chapman (1832–1909)

—— Homer Montgomery (1838–1924)
Married Elizabeth Willey (1842–1902)

—— William H. H. Montgomery (1840–before 1920)
Married Eugenie Herbert (1845–1920)

This chart has been edited to show only those children of Abraham Montgomery and Permelia Norris who are discussed in the book. Children not shown on the chart include Elizabeth, Josephine, and Hannah.

well as news about their respective regiments in the field.

When, on July 22, 1861, President Lincoln, in response to the Union defeat at the battle of Bull Run, issued his urgent call for an additional five hundred thousand men to enlist in the Union army for three years, Mary Ann Montgomery felt an overwhelming fear for her family.

Much to her dismay, Mary Ann's brother George was talking about enlisting in the Thirty-ninth Ohio that was recruiting in the county. Her cousins Homer and Ellis Montgomery had already enlisted on July 16 in Company A of the Thirty-ninth. Charles Montgomery had also enlisted on the same day and in the same company, but the paternity and relationship of the twenty-three-year-old Scioto County native to the rest of the Montgomery family had been the source of speculation and gossip, which had not yielded any satisfactory explanation. But the details of Charles Montgomery's birth were of no concern to Mary Ann. She knew, deep in her heart, that her husband would feel honor bound to respond as well.

## Montgomery Men at War

Mary Ann's fears were realized when on August 5, 1861, her husband, McLain, and her youngest brother, James, enlisted as privates in Company A of the Thirty-third Ohio Volunteer Infantry. She was proud of her family, yet felt ashamed that her own selfish desires perpetually intruded upon her thoughts. She flinched slightly when the movement of the child she carried in her belly announced its own imminent arrival. How would she ever manage? How could he leave her now? How could these forces over which she was so powerless interrupt a life that seemed so full of promise and happiness? It seemed that she had no control over her own emotions that erupted into tears on a daily basis. How she hated this damnable rebellion that had intruded into their lives!

Three weeks later, on August 27, her husband and her brother were mustered into the regiment at Camp Morrow in Portsmouth, Ohio. McLain was promoted to sergeant that same day and for the remainder of August and all of September the male members of her family were absorbed with their new responsibilities of training, drilling, and learning the essentials of military life midst the usual oppressive heat and humidity so common to the area in late summer. On those rare occasions when the men had an opportunity for a brief return home, they described in great detail the intricacies of their newly acquired skills. They were buoyed by their experiences and were filled with pride for what they were about to do for their country. Again, Mary Ann felt a tinge of guilt because she resented her husband's apparent eagerness to leave her and the child they were about to have. Although he repeatedly assured her of his love and of his concern for her, he left no doubt that his duty was clear and he was determined to fulfill it. To Mary Ann, her duty was clear as well.

On Saturday, October 12, 1861, Mary Ann and McLain Montgomery became the proud parents of a baby girl, whom they named Ella. For a brief moment, the newborn child was gift enough to lift

| | | | | |
|---|---|---|---|---|
| Sons of William Montgomery, Jr. Enlisted in Scioto County, Ohio | | | | |
| *Name* | *Age* | *Rank* | *Company* | *Regiment* |
| George | 26 | Pvt. | A | 39th OVI |
| James | 19 | Pvt. | A | 33rd OVI |
| Sons of Abraham Montgomery Enlisted in Scioto County, Ohio | | | | |
| Homer | 20 | Sgt. | A | 39th OVI |
| Ellis | 31 | Pvt. | A | 39th OVI |
| William H.H. | 30 | Pvt. | E | 140th OVI |
| Son of Margaret Swyers and unknown father Enlisted in Scioto County, Ohio | | | | |
| Charles | 23 | Pvt. | A | 39th OVI |
| Sons of John B. Montgomery Enlisted in Scioto County, Ohio | | | | |
| McLain | 28 | Sgt. | A | 33rd OVI |
| Sons of John B. Montgomery Enlisted in Bureau County Illinois | | | | |
| Thaddeus D. | 35 | Bugler | B | 64th Ill. Inf. |
| Isaac Newton | 35 | Pvt. | I | 31st Ill. Inf. |

Mary Ann's spirits. However, two days later, Monday, October 14, her husband gave them both a parting kiss and returned to Portsmouth to rejoin the regiment. Later that day, her sisters, Cynthia and Sarah, and her mother, Nancy, traveled to the wharf to watch McLain and James as they and their regiment departed.

Upon their return to Wheelersburg, Cynthia and Sarah were eager to share with Mary Ann the excitement they had witnessed in town. There had been a parade of the regiment from Camp Morrow to the wharf as a band played and the citizens loudly cheered their departing heroes. It was an impressive sight as they boarded the *Bostonas*, the two steamers that would take them to Maysville, Kentucky. They described for her the officers who were so striking in their uniforms. They were particularly impressed with the twenty-nine-year-old colonel, Joshua Woodrow Sill, a West Point graduate from Chillicothe, Ohio, who would command the regiment. He looked so young, yet so polished and self-confident, especially as compared to forty-four-year-old Lt. Col. Oscar F. Moore, second in command. Moore had enjoyed a good reputation as a local political leader, but clearly did not have the military bearing of the young Sill.

To Mary Ann, it appeared that the whole world was almost giddy with excitement, while she found herself in what she believed to be, life's lowest ebb. She resented the fact that her sisters still had their husbands at home to care for them and their children. She could not comprehend their apparent indifference to her situation. They were quick to point out to her that she was fortunate that her mother, Nancy, was there in her home to help her, but this was no comfort. She felt absolutely alone.

## Illinois Response

When the Civil War broke out, robust outdoorsman Del Montgomery enlisted early on November 1, 1861, in Company B of the Sixty-fourth Illinois Infantry known as Yates Sharpshooters. Younger brother Newton felt pressure from his brothers and friends to enlist. In addition to five stepchildren, the couple had three daughters of their own by 1862, and Newton's financial status remained unchanged and he was still work-

*Del Montgomery*

ing as a farm laborer. This coupled with the perpetual complaints from his wife, regarding his inability to provide adequately for the family's needs, were a constant source of friction. Despite his rather frail constitution and his susceptibility to seasonal illness, he finally decided to enlist December 30, 1863, in Company I of the Thirty-first Illinois. This company was composed primarily of men from Bureau County. Much to his wife's dismay, her eighteen-year-old son, James

H. Robinson, enlisted two months later in Company D, of the Thirty-fourth Illinois Infantry. Newton's wife placed responsibility for her son's decision to join the army squarely on the shoulders of her husband. It was a burden that would weigh heavily.

## *Letters from the Front*

McLain wrote his first letter home on October 27, just two weeks after the regiment's departure from Portsmouth, bound for Camp Kenton in Maysville, Kentucky. There, they were under the command of Brig. Gen. William "Bull" Nelson. From Maysville they marched south through eastern Kentucky to the town of Hazel Green in Wolfe County where they arrived at four o'clock in the morning on October 23. The Fifth Kentucky C.S.A. under Col. John S. Williams had been recruiting in the area and Nelson's men were assigned to drive them out of Kentucky and into Virginia.

Mary Ann was excited upon receiving her first letter from her husband, but it was with a certain amount of trepidation that she opened it and began to read, uncertain as to whether the news would be good or bad. She had no idea what to expect.

Sergeant Montgomery's letter indicated a fair degree of excitement and pride in the regiment's first foray into the field, and he had quickly incorporated the soldier's parlance for the secessionist rebels (Sesech) into his account.

Hazel green, Wolfe County, Kentucky Oct. 27th, 1861

Dear wife, I take the first opportunity to write you a few lines. I have not had a chance to write before since I left Portsmouth. We have had a pretty hard march. We started from Maysville on the 16th and arrived here on the 25, a distance of 95 miles over the worst road I ever saw, but we are now in good quarters. The Cesech [Secessionists] left every thing in our possession. We have taken about 90 horses and about as many beef cattle. We have had no fight yet but once in a while we exchange shots with a straggler. We have a number of prisoners and the rebels have got three of our men. Hazelgreen is about as big as Wheelersburgh, and there is but two families here. The rest all left on short notice. We have mills to grind our corn, stoves to bake it and everything we could ask for and if I could be certain that you and baby was well I would [be] as well content as I ever can be away from home.

I have no idea when I will be at home but you may rest assured that I will come as soon as possible but my time is short and I must wind up with telling you that James and me are both well and God grant that this may find you and my little darling enjoying alike the same blessing. Kiss the little cub 1000 times for me, but save a few for me when I come. Tell mother that the Cesesh can beat her raising sweet potatoes all holler, and I know just how to cook them and the Kentucky Shangheid chickens are just as fat as any on Dogwood ridge and full as plenty. Now good by Mary till I have [a] chance to write again answer this as soon as you can. Direct your letter thus

To Mclain Montgomery
Co. A, 33rd Regt. O.V.I
By the way of Mount Sterling, Ky.
In care of Capt. S.A. Currie

In the same letter, Sergeant Montgomery sent along a brief note to Mary's brother, George, who was still at home, but no doubt feeling pressure that he too should answer his country's call.

A few lines to George. We are about 3000 strong and daily strengthening our force. Hazelgreen is situated on Red River in just about as hilly a country as you ever saw. Our rout[e] here lays through Mason, Bath and Fleming and Montgomery Counties. We are now in Wolfe. The first 2 days travel lay through the finest country I ever saw and from that time on we found nothing but mountains with here and an old deserted Cesesh farm. Chickens, hogs and cattle all left behind. Companies C and E arrived here about 2 o'clock in the morning. The inhabitants left and then the work of plunder commenced. 2 stores and every dwelling was ransacked from top to bottom. We took a stand of bees and have been living on honey for a few days. I don't know when we leave here nor where we go when we do leave. We are all well equipped and anxious for a fight. We have six pieces of cannon and a company of cavalry. Don't forget to write. Good by.

Mc Montgomery to George Montgomery
Direct Co. A 33rd O.V.U.S.

Via Mount Sterling, Montgomery Co., Ky.
In care of Capt. S. A. Currie

After a brief respite in Hazel Green, the regiment continued southward on November 7, toward Piketon, Kentucky (now Pikeville), where they successfully routed the Confederate troops at Ivy Mountain and drove them out of Kentucky through Pound Gap into Virginia. Near the end of November, they marched from Piketon to Louisa on the Big Sandy River, boarded steamers and traveled to Louisville, Kentucky. From Louisville they continued on the Louisville to Nashville Railroad about fifty miles south to Bacon Creek, Kentucky, where they went into winter quarters.

In camp, things suddenly took a turn for the worse. Although their march into eastern Kentucky had resulted in success without the loss of a single man to enemy fire, their first winter at Bacon Creek was filled with misery, sickness, and death.

The regiment had gone into the field in October with 880 men. At Bacon Creek the location chosen for the camp was less than adequate. The camp was situated in a low-lying basin surrounded by higher land and ridges that drained into the soil, groundwater, and creeks. Lt. Angus Waddle of the Thirty-third had described the area as "a perfect mudhole."

The result, of course, was a high level of disease, which included the predominant diarrhea and dysentery as well as measles and small pox. On December 24, 1861, there were 276 men sick in camp and in the hospital. Seventeen men from the Thirty-third died in the month of December alone, and eight more would die in early January.

Mary Ann had received only one letter from her husband since his departure from Portsmouth. That first letter had been filled with his exuberance over their successful drive into eastern Kentucky, but now, two months later she had received no word from him. She was sick with worry especially since other neighbors had learned of the unhealthy conditions and the number of deaths at the regiment's new camp. Finally, in mid-December, Sergeant Montgomery, wrote to his wife and offered a variety of circumstances that had prevented him from writing.

From Louisville, Kentucky Dec. 16th, 1861

Dear wife. I will try and write a few lines to let you know my circumstances which I dared not do before. I expected to get a furlough when I landed here. Then we was promised our pay. I thought when I got my money I would certainly come home, but the next day I was taken sick. I was taken to the camp hospital where [I] got worse very fast. There was about four days I thought I could not live, but I am very week and must quit. I will not get my money till next payday. Tell W.D. Corns [Wesley C. Corns, a river pilot, neighbor and friend] to send me two or three dollars for I need a little very bad. Good Bye Dear May. Kiss baby for me and give my love to all.

Mc Montgomery to Mary Montgomery

Please direct your letters to U.S. General Hospital Corner of 9th & Broadway, Louisville, Kentucky

Two days later, Sergeant Montgomery asked Maj. Joshua Van-Zandt Robinson to write to Mary to reassure her that her husband was indeed recovering.

Louisville, Kentucky,
December 18th 1861
Mrs. Mary Montgomery
Wheelersburg, Ohio

Madam:

Your husband has been sick, but is now rapidly recovering. He was paid today, and requests me to send you thirty dollars which you will please find enclosed.

Very Respectfully
J. V. Robinson, Jr.
Major, 33 Regt. O.V. U.S.A.

Christmas 1861 passed, and was a melancholy one at home. Little Ella, now just two months old, was unaware of the many lonely, sleepless nights that her mother quietly wept and worried about her husband. She had begged him to seek a furlough so that he might fully recover at home. In response Sergeant Montgomery appealed to Capt. Samuel A. Currie, Company A, for help in securing a furlough.

Louisville, Ky. Dec. 29th 1861

Dear Captain, I take this opportunity of writing you a few lines to let you know how I am prospering. I left the hospital a week ago today and came to a private house where I have been treated very kindly. I do not wish to intrude on their hospitality longer than I can help. I am now able to take short walks about the city and I could very well stand a trip home. So captain, if you will try and procure me a furlough I will be under many obligations to you and I will give you my honor that I will join my regiment as soon as I am able So please captain do all for me you can if you can do any for me. Don't direct to the hospital, but to Louisville so it will stop at the post office. Let me know how James is getting along and do what you can for me soon. I shall not try to write any more for I don't expect you can read all that I have written. Good bye

McLain Montgomery
To Capt. S. A. Currie

Sergeant Montgomery was granted a thirty-day furlough during the month of January 1862 and returned home for a much sought after reunion with his wife and his first opportunity to spend a little time with his two and a half month old daughter, Ella.

# CHAPTER 5

# *Into Tennessee and Alabama 1862*

Mary Ann had been grateful for the brief time she and Ella had enjoyed with her husband during the month of January. But already, she missed him and the emptiness she felt seemed even more intense than before. She was startled by the knock at the door but was delighted that her neighbor, John McAlier had just returned from his visit to Camp Madison, Kentucky, and brought with him welcome news from McLain. It was not unusual for people to visit the camps, and she looked forward to hearing her neighbor's views on conditions at the front. But that would have to wait. The letter he carried in his hand was her first priority. As she read, she was once again aware of her husband's excitement and eager anticipation for what might lie ahead. Those were not the emotions that consumed her thoughts, as fears for her husband's safety were uppermost in her mind.

Dear wife

I have but a few minutes to write for we are ordered to be ready to march in thirty minutes. Every thing is confusion. The boys are all most wild with excitement. We expect to go straight to Bowling Green where we expect to have a big fight. The news came to camp tonight that Columbus [on the Mississippi River in Hickman County, Kentucky] was taken but we doubt it. I got to camp Jefferson last Saturday and on Monday morning and came to camp Madison near Munfordsville. James is well and so am I, and if I know that you and Ella was well I would be very well satisfied. McAlier is here and is going to start home in the morning. I will send this by him but I must quit for I have to go to work. I have been on duty today or I would have wrote you a long letter. Give my love to mother and all who may enquire. Kiss Ella for me and write to me soon. Direct your letter to Mundfordsville, Kentucky in care of Capt. Currie Co. A 33rd O.V. U.S.A. good by, God bless you

McLain Montgomery
To Mary Montgomery

In a little over a week, Mary Ann received another letter from McLain. This had been written just two days after his last and she was struck by its melancholy mood. She smiled as she read the four lines from the poem, *The Soldier's Dream,* by Scottish poet, Thomas Campbell, and noted that her husband had written an abbreviated version and was confused as to its author. The important thing to Mary Ann, however, was that he shared her love for literature and chose these words to express his feelings.

Feb. 12, 1862
Camp J.Q. Adams

"The Soldiers dream of Home
At the dead of the night a sweet vision I saw,
And thrice e'er the morning I dreamt it again,
But sorrow return'd with the dawning of morn,
And the voice in my dreaming ear melted away."
Bryant

Dear wife,

I wrote to you while I was at camp Madison and thought I should have an answer by this time, but I find I was mistaken. I have dreamed of home every night since I left. The verse at the top of this page gives my experience better than I can give it in my own words. Last night while I dreamed, I walked in the sunshine of spring with my Ella and Mary by my side and I was happy, but morning came and dispelled the happy vision and I found myself five miles on the Nashville side of Bowling Green, the sky overcast with clouds and the rain pouring down which it continues to do up to this time, 11 o'clock, and no prospect of any better weather. I am well at present and I am so well content as I ever can be away from home.

I suppose you have heard that Bowling Green was taken without the loss of a man. Bowling green is a beautiful place situated in as fine a scope of county as I ever saw. But the town and country is greatly reduced by the rebels. I passed within 7 miles of the Mammoth Cave and within a mile and a half of Diamond Cave and I saw Sinking Creek. Quite a curiosity. The stream runs between very high banks when it suddenly loses itself near 100 ft. under ground and there is a mill in the mouth of the cave where the creek loses itself and does not make its appearance again for the distance of five miles where it empties into Barren River.

But I must this scroll to a close for I have another letter to write to pay for this paper envelope and stamp. James is well and in good spirits. Tell George that our next move will be toward Nashville. Our way is clear and we don't expect to tarry long before we reach Memphis when I expect the war will be pretty well wound up. Then I hope I can come home and realize the bright visions that come to me while wrapped in the slumbers of midnight in the tented field. Give my love to Mother but keep a good share for yourself and Ella. Kiss Ella many, many times and save a good supply for your ever loving husband. Farewell Mary, God bless you.

Mc Montgomery
To Mary Montgomery

McLain's dilemma regarding the scarcity of writing materials was a common one; however, he was fortunate that he was able to obtain the necessary items by writing letters for those who could not write their own. Although mail delivery was slow and unreliable, it was more efficient than the arrival of the paymaster. It was not unusual for the army to be two or three months behind in paying the men. Sergeant Montgomery, like many soldiers, withheld only a small portion of his pay and sent the greater amount home to his family.

March 7, 1862

Camp A. Jackson

Dear wife, It was with pleasure I received and read your letter, which came to hand yesterday. Nothing could have pleased me better than the welcome news that you and my darling Ella was in good health except being at home with you of course. I am getting fat as a pig and twice as hearty. We are encamped five miles east of Nashville. We have done some very hard marching since I joined the reg't, and I stood it much better than I expected on our march here. We passed through some of the finest country I ever saw. We have not done no fighting and don't expect to do any so you need not fret about my safety unless the Lord should cut short my existence by disease or some other natural cause.

Our Colonel [Joshua W. Sill] thinks we will be home by the middle of summer and I hope we will for to me there is no place like home although I am as well content here as I can be under the circumstances. Tell George that I will write to him as soon as I can find any thing of interest to write about. I suppose you have got the letter that I wrote while at Bowling Green by this time so that there is nothing new to write unless I recount the bad weather and the late fatigue of our march here.

We left our camp at Bowling Green on the 23rd of Feb. and marched 15 miles to the town of Franklin during the heaviest kind of rain. We started the next morning but very little refreshed and foot sore enough and marched 14 miles farther, but the weather was fine. We camped at night in an open field. The evening warm enough to sleep without blankets but before morning it was blowing cold enough to freeze but we left early and marched 24 miles and camped 6 miles north of Nashville. The weather still cold and we not much better rested. I assure you we lay that night on the ground without any tents. The next morning about 3 o'clock we was on the march for Nashville when within an hour's march of that place as tired as we were, we was ordered back two miles. Here we camped two days after which we came through Nashville to where we now are. Yesterday it snowed and blowed very hard. Today the weather is very fine but for the want of paper I must quit. Yesterday I received two months pay, 34 dollars. 30 you will find enclosed. Write soon. Give my love to mother and all who may enquire and may God bless and protect you and my Ella.

Once again the days seemed to drag by while the nights were unbearably long as she waited for another letter. A little over three weeks after his letter from Camp Jackson, McLain finally wrote again.

Camp Van Buren, Tennessee
March 30th 1862

Dear wife. I received your kind letter yesterday; and it would be impossible for [me] to give you any idea of the pleasure I experienced while reading it. It was like sunshine in winter dispelling the gloom and scattering the clouds, which seemed to hang like an "ignis fatres" [*sic*] over my pathway of life.

Mary smiled at her husband's use of the Latin phrase *ignis fatuus*, and understood immediately that he, like her, often felt despondent over the deep loneliness they shared at being apart. It was an expression often used locally to denote some mystical phenomenon that was responsible for unexplainable events. To Mary Ann, the entire catastrophe of war seemed the result of some unknown evil that disrupted the lives of ordinary people and threw them into chaos.

Not that I am complaining Mary for the prospects is brighter than they ever have been since I left home. But Mary it is so long between times that I hear from you. The every day life of the soldier becomes a drudge, but the precious letter bearing the welcome news of your welfare at home makes me cheerful and my duties light. The birds sing sweeter, the sun shines bright and everything seems inspired with new life since the reception of that silent messenger assured me that all was well. Dear Mary I am many miles from home and in a strange country and surrounded with people of every caste of character and every thing calculated to divert the mind or attract attention, but my heart is absent. It is at home with you and my beloved Ella. Ella God bless her if there ever was a being on earth that I could worship it is that sweet child and I pray to God that our political sky will soon clear up and let me come home and then I never expect to be separated from my Dear Mary and Ella again until the final separation of all that is earthly.

Every letter provided countless hours of comfort. She read each one, over and over and even read them to little Ella. And, when her husband expressed confidence that the war would soon be over, she was filled with such joy that daily chores no longer seemed such an insurmountable burden.

> *I* can't believe like Hungerford [Sgt. James C. Hungerford, Company E] that we will have a chance to carry our next pay home, that is unless we keep it a good while. But I think the day is not far distant when we will come. James says he intends to carry his own letter next time and save postage. He thinks like Hungerford that we will start for home before many days. We will be paid again in a day or two and then I will write again, but I can't trust money in a letter from here yet. The mail is not safe, but Smith Patingale [Private Company F] is about to get a discharge and I will send it by him.

> We are now camped about one mile west of Murfresboro and twenty-nine east of Nashville. We are building bridges across Stone River that the Cesesh burnt down. When we leave here we expect to go to Decatur, Alabama. Cannonading has been heard in a southwest direction for the last three days. Where it is we don't know.

Mary Ann hoped that her husband's expectations to move deeper into Confederate territory to Alabama were wrong. It seemed to her that the farther south the regiment went, the greater the danger to the men.

> The weather is warm and pleasant. The trees begin to look green and things in general show that spring is here. The first peach blossoms was seen on the 18th, hyacinths the same day. We saw the first palmetto here and went a fishing for the first time this season, but caught nothing.

> Major J. V. Robinson is dead and it is expected that Capt. S.A. Currie will assume the majorship of the Regt.

Folks at home were saddened by the news of the death of Maj. Joshua Vanzandt Robinson of Portsmouth, Ohio. Many were aware that he had been plagued by poor health throughout most of his life. Mary Ann was frustrated by the fact that she could no longer pay for a newspaper. Luckily, however, sometimes neighbors, such as John Kennedy, would share with her news from the *Portsmouth Times*. On March 1 the paper had carried the report of the major's illness at

Bacon Creek and had announced his return to Portsmouth on Wednesday, February 26, to recuperate at home. The news of his death at home on March 23, 1862, had also been reported.

> ☞ MAJOR J. V. ROBINSON, of the 33rd Ohio, arrived at home on Wednesday morning last. The health of the Major is very precarious, and has compelled him to leave his post.

*The* Portsmouth Times, *Saturday, March 1, 1862.*

I send with this letter a Nashville paper thinking perhaps it may interest you. I am truly sorry that your paper fails to come for I fear now it will never come without another dollar. Your postage stamps come to hand all right. Without them I would not be able to send this letter. They are worth 5 cts. a piece here and not to be had at that so I will have to depend on you for them, but don't send more than 5 at a time and then if lost it will not be much, but I must come to a close hoping that this will find you enjoying as good health as the writer. Give my love to mother and tell her that I will try and prevail on James to write again soon Good bye Dear Mary. Kiss my darling Ella for me and write soon. I now leave you in the care of a merciful God, hoping to hear from you soon.
From your affectionate husband Mc Montgomery

## Celebration and Dismay

Mary Ann's younger brother George was as eager as she for any news about the war and he would patiently wait for permission to read McLain's letters. Although these letters contained much that was of a very personal nature, Mary Ann gladly shared them. Everyone in the family was keenly aware that George felt that he too had an obligation to enlist.

Her brother, who was rather shy by nature, had always been uncomfortable in the company of women, and his own sisters enjoyed watching his embarrassment when they teased him about the matter. The situation was about to change, however, when, in June of 1860, eighteen-year-old Mary Catharine Modes, daughter of Christian Modes, a native of Germany and a weaver by trade, moved to Wheelersburg. The Montgomery women took note of the fact that George had become more diligent in his church attendance and often dallied after the service to chat with Mary Catharine. Before long, George was seen walking her home. Over the next few months, George often enjoyed invitations to the Modes' household for dinner. Finally, in early spring of 1862, George proudly announced that he and Mary Catharine were about to get hitched. It was an announcement greeted with great joy by the Montgomery family. On April 27, 1862, twenty-six-year-old George and Mary Catharine were wed and the festivities in celebration of the event provided a mood of gaiety.

That celebratory feeling soon gave way to concern and fear for family on the battlefield. By late June there was still no word from either McLain or James about the Thirty-third and its activities. However, local newspapers carried accounts of the raid led by civilian James J. Andrews and twenty-two men of Sill's brigade into Georgia to steal a locomotive on the Western and Atlantic Railroad. It was a mission that resulted in the capture of all of those involved. There was widespread outrage at the news that Andrews and seven of the men had been tried and executed. These tidbits of information only served to intensify family concerns.

Earlier that year, Cousin Ellis had been discharged from Company A of the Thirty-ninth Ohio on a surgeon's certificate of disability and returned home suffering from tuberculosis. He died from this devastating disease in November of 1862. Cousin Homer was still with the Thirty-ninth and had seen action at the siege of Corinth, Mississippi, in April and May. George's sense of obligation to serve was heightened by his cousins' experiences. On August 14, 1862, George, like his cousins Homer and Ellis had done a year earlier, enlisted in Company A of the Thirty-ninth Ohio Infantry.

Although Mary wrote to her husband to describe the events at home, the happiness that she had enjoyed and the optimism she had felt from McLain's letter of March 30, slowly faded as days, then weeks, and finally months passed without further word from her husband. Mail delivery between Ohio and the regiment was delayed by several weeks as the regiment moved further south. It may have been that Sergeant Montgomery dutifully wrote to Mary on a regular basis over the course of the next five months but the letters were either lost or intercepted by the rebels. Whatever the situation, Mary Ann was consumed with fear, and expected at any moment to learn that her husband had been killed. She inquired of friends and neighbors for any news they might have from family members in the regiment. She scoured all local newspapers she could find, but still received no news to ease her worries. She would not receive another letter from him for what seemed an eternity.

## Seizing the Rails

The rumor Sergeant Montgomery had mentioned regarding their movement deep into the Confederacy proved to be true. While Andrews and the raiders carried out their part of the plan, McLain and James along with the rest of Sill's brigade moved to Huntsville, Alabama, to seize control of the Memphis to Charleston Railroad.

There is no record of Sergeant Montgomery's thoughts or opinions about these operations for there are no letters between March 30 and September 8. The regiment had been constantly on the move along the line of the railroad from April through the month of May. During that time their mail was destroyed on two occasions by raids by Confederate troops. On yet another occasion, the men of the Thirty-third Ohio were distressed to learn that their provision train, their mail and the guard accompanying the train were captured in early May by Capt. John Hunt Morgan's men near Columbia, Tennessee. Morgan paroled the guard of about two hundred men, kept the supplies for his own troops, and sent the mail back to Nashville with his compliments.

Raids by Confederate cavalry which intercepted mail and provision trains continued throughout the rest of May of 1862 as the Thirty-third Ohio attempted to capture the Confederate raiders. And, as Lt. Angus Waddle from the Thirty-third noted, "It is not much use to send infantry after cavalry, especially where every cross road is well known to the latter." During this time the regiment, on the march through the mountains of Tennessee, had no baggage, no tents and no opportunities to write or receive mail.

Sill's Brigade as part of General Mitchel's division continued to control the Memphis and Charleston Railroad from April 11 until early June when they were ordered into Tennessee in an unsuccessful attempt to seize control of Chattanooga. In July, after the reassignment of General Mitchel to South Carolina and reorganization of command structure, the Thirty-third was under Maj. Gen. Alexander McDowell McCook's First Army Corps. They were ordered to the mouth of Battle Creek near Jasper, Tennessee.

## Defense of Fort McCook

Their assignment was to construct a fort on the side of a mountain near the Tennessee River. This was in response to heightened concerns that Confederate general Braxton Bragg was moving with a large force into eastern Tennessee. After constructing the fort, the Thirty-third went into regular quarters about a mile from the fort along the banks of the river. By mid-August, Confederate troops were camped on the opposite side of the river.

Over the course of the next week, General Buell ordered the dispatch of additional troops to Bridgeport, and personally restricted all furloughs insisting that he needed every man available. On August 21, the remaining troops, which consisted of only four companies of the Thirty-third and two companies of the Fourth Ohio Cavalry, were ordered to occupy the fort. On August 27, they received word that Confederate troops were massing to cross the Tennessee River at Bridgeport. In response, a small detachment of cavalry was ordered to prevent their crossing. About noon, just as the cavalry was engaging forces at Bridgeport, a Confederate battery of three guns opened fire on the fort. It was an encounter, which required them to ultimately abandon the fort under cover of darkness.

The following letter was written nearly two weeks after their encounter with Confederate troops under the command of Brig. Gen. Samuel Bell Maxey, C.S.A. at Fort McCook. Sergeant Montgomery described the experiences on August 27.

Those five long months without a single letter from her beloved husband seemed like an eternity. When the precious letter finally arrived, it was again with much anxiety that Mary opened it. The agony of separation along with a thousand imagined disasters had flooded her mind for the past five months. Was he injured, or worse yet, had he been killed? Did he still love her as she loved him? What terrible truth would the letter reveal?

As she began to read its contents, she felt the panic begin to rise. Through her husbands words she could sense the danger he had faced, and she could never be certain that he was unharmed. For if he were well, would he not have realized how anxious she had been. The letter seemed so matter of fact, so full of detail, but she could not understand how he could appear to be so unaware of her feelings after enduring so many months without a letter from him.

Louisville, Sept. 8, 1862

Dear Wife, You think I have forgotten you but I know you will forgive me when you hear the circumstances. The last time I wrote I was near Battle Creek, Tenn. At the time we had a force of about 30,000. About the 18th of Aug. the forces were drawn up and left our reg't and a part of the Fourth Ohio Cavalry in possession of Fort McCook. We held under [/] away until the 26. That morning we placed a heavy guard on the wall of the fort to keep up appearances. Night came and darkness shut out the sight. The rebel pickets which had been in ear shot all day were quiet. I was on guard at the time by myself and while I was alone by the water's edge, I was thinking of home and of those I love. Nothing but the monotonous call of the sleepy sentinel of " all is well". occurred to break my dreamy reflection. I thought of our position here in sight of the enemy with the river between us and no guns larger than a musket to defend our selves. The thought came over me that the cry of all is well might be changed and the slogan of the battle field take its place, but the night passed quietly a way and I felt relieved when the light of morning came. But still a foreboding of evil possessed me.

James went on picket that morning and I went to my tent to rest About nine o'clock word came that our wagon train was attacked by the rebel cavalry and we sent a division of the 33rd to relieve them. They drove them in and encountered a battalion of infantry and was compelled to fall back. About that time a battery of three guns opened on us firing about fifteen shots per minute. One was a twelve pounder. The other two 6 pounders. The 12-pound gun fed us on grape canister and shell. The other kept time with shot and small shells. The second shell that came bursted in our quarters. A portion of it passed through my tent and whistled uncomfortable close to my ears. Our company formed and passed through a perfect shower of shot and shell, but fortunately none of us was hurt. After dodging a while, our Co. [A] and Co. B was ordered out in an open field to guard against cavalry. Again the gauntlet had to be run but we passed through safe a second time and took up our position in line in full view of the enemy. But it was not long before they began to make our position very uncomfortable. We would watch the flash of the guns and lie down until the storm passed. Some came so close if we had been standing we could not have escaped. No cavalry made their appearance. We was ordered out on pickett where for the present we was safe.

Sergeant Montgomery did not mention in his letter the precautions taken to help safeguard their midnight departure from the fort. Small detachments of some of their best marksmen armed with Enfield rifles were ordered to the banks of the river to engage those manning the batteries. They were successful in forcing the rebels to move their artillery back a short distance. In addition, Colonel Harris ordered that the remaining men in the fort tear up tents into strips that were wrapped around the wheels of the wagons to muffle their sound. It was, no doubt due to these measures, that they were able to evacuate the fort without heavy losses.

At 12 o'clock at night we was ordered to start for Winchester, a distance (?) miles. We had to pass again before the enemy's guns but just as we started it commenced raining very hard, otherwise we must have suffered greatly for the range was short being less than 1000 yds. Dark as it was there was but one shot fired while we were passing. They still kept up the fire until about noon the next day, not being aware that we had left. We marched that night and next day 28 miles and camped on the Cumberland Mountain with our blankets and very little to eat having left our tents and everything else behind. My loss was 15 dollars, but that was light compared to others. The next day we reached Dechard Station, 15 miles. Rested 2 days and marched to Tulahoma, distance 15 miles. Next day we reached Wartrace distance 25 miles. Next day we reached Murfreesboro, 25 miles. Next day within 5 miles Nashville. Rested one day then marched night and day until we reached this place tired and thirsty enough. How long we stay I don't know. I hope long enough to get rested. On our way here, I stood picket within sight of Bragg's pickets. We exchanged several shots with them but with no effect.

She realized that conditions at the front were perilous, but was disappointed that her husband expressed no concerns about life at home and about the challenges of maintaining the farm and the fall harvest with nearly all able bodied men being at war.

Now Mary I want you to write to me and tell me how you and my darling Ella is getting along. Give my love to mother and all who may enquire. Now Dear Mary, do not give yourself any trouble on my account, for in spite of all the hardships, I am well. James is well and appears to improve. He has changed very much within the last year. Good bye Dear Mary. Kiss my Ella for me. Save one good kiss for me if I am lucky enough to get home. Good bye. God bless you. Direct to Louisville, 33rd.

## The 39th Ohio and 64th Illinois at Corinth, Mississippi, September 1862

Mary Ann Montgomery treasured every letter she received from family during the war and preserved them in her collection. She received the following from her brother George shortly after his joining his regiment, the Thirty-ninth Ohio Infantry under the command of Col. John Groesbeck of Cincinnati, Ohio. This regiment was comprised mainly of men from Hamilton County, Ohio, but there were also parts of companies from Athens, Clinton, Clermont, Washington, and Highland counties. Company A was recruited in Scioto County and Hamilton County.

In the fall of 1862, the Thirty-ninth Ohio was attached to Col. John W. Fuller's First Brigade, of the Second Division, Army of Mississippi under the command of Maj. Gen. William S. Rosecrans who had succeeded Brig. Gen. John Pope on June 26 of that year. On September 19 the Army of the Mississippi engaged the Confederate Army of the West under Maj. Gen. Sterling Price at Iuka. On that day the performance of the Union forces was unimpressive and seemed to lack cohesiveness and coordination, and failed to produce a decisive victory. Fortunately, Price decided to disengage and retreat. Price's plan was to join Confederate Army of Tennessee under Maj. Gen. Earl Van Dorn and to plan the battle of Corinth for the following month.

Twenty-six-year-old Pvt. George Montgomery, following the battle of Corinth, Mississippi, fought on October 3 and 4, 1862, wrote to share with his family news of his first combat experience

*George Montgomery*

After the first day of fighting, Confederate forces had successfully driven the Union troops back; however, an over confident Van Dorn decided to postpone any further operations until the next day. The following day, a series of unforeseen events postponed the Confederate attack allowing Union forces to regroup and launch a heavy, concentrated artillery barrage upon the rebels and eventually forced Van Dorn into a full retreat. Confederate losses during the battle were 4,233 men, which was about double the number of Union casualties.

Fuller's brigade included the Twenty-seventh Ohio, which had been organized by Colonel Fuller and was composed of men from various parts of the state with companies E, F, and G including men from the Hanging Rock regions of Scioto, Jackson, Gallia, and Lawrence counties. Knowing that folks at home would be interested in any news regarding local soldiers, George included reports of casualties from the Twenty-seventh.

October 14th 1862
Corinth Mississippi
Dear Sister,

I take my seat this morning to inform you that I am well and hearty and hope that you are the same. We have had a hard battle here and we gained the day with a great victory on the fourth (&) fifth and then we went after them on their retreat and General Herbert, [apparently a reference to Brig. Gen. Stephen A. Hurlburt, commanding Fourth Division, Right Wing, Army of the Tennessee] one of our Generals, cut Price's army to pieces and then we turned back to this place. We have been doing heavy marching since [we] have been here, and I think that we will not stay here long. . . . I received two letters from you last night and was glad to hear from you and hear that you was well.

You stated in your letter that you wanted to know how I sent you that locket. I sent it by mail from Cincinnati before I left. I'm glad to hear that you heard from James and Mc that they were at Louisville. I suppose that Rose[crans] will be a long before long for I don't know what keeps them so long. I am this [night] on guard, very hot and cool nights. We have had a hard rain Friday the seventh and I was in all of the storm which was very hard on the men. I think this is a hard country in this part of the state and a general thing the weather is bad.

Mr. Web, [1st Lt. Henry A. Webb, Company G, 27th Ohio Volunteer Infantry] the man that was manager of the Howard Furness was killed dead and Harve Fullerton [Sgt. J. H. Fullerton, Company G, 27th Ohio] was wounded in the arm. This was the hardest battle that was fought in this the western army. We have heard that there was a great many soldiers coming down the river, but we have not heard where to. I hope some of them will come here.

John Mooney [Private, Company A, 39th Ohio Infantry] is not well. I think a letter from his wife [Annettunia Wolfin Mooney] would help him some for he is out all patience. He has not heard from his family since he left. He sends his best wishes to you all. I must come to a close for this time. My wish is [to] write soon. Give my best respects to all of my friends who enquires about me. Good by. Direct your letter to Corinth, Mississippi in care of Lieutenant [William P.] Newman Co. A. 39th Reg. Ohio.

Tell our friends to write for we are glad to hear from home by some of them. No more at present from your brother, George Montgomery.

George Montgomery was not the only member of the family to see action at Corinth. Cousin Del, serving with Company B of the Sixty-fourth Illinois Infantry also fought in the battle. The Sixty-fourth had been present at Iuka in September, but had not been engaged. At Corinth, the regiment was heavily engaged and on the second day of fighting suffered the loss of seventy men, killed, wounded and missing, One of those injured was Pvt. Thaddeus Delorain Montgomery.

On Saturday, October 4, Del Montgomery was struck in the chest by a partially spent ball. Apparently the wound was not a deep one, and the surgeons on the field felt that it was not dangerous, but it had produced a burn and left shrapnel fragments imbedded in the wound. Del's condition continued to deteriorate and, in December, regimental surgeon Jarod T. Stewart sent him to Jackson, Tennessee, to recuperate. He was finally discharged on a surgeon's certificate of disability on March 3, 1863.

## Battle of Chaplin Hills at Perryville, Kentucky

On October 6, Mary had begun a letter to her husband, but as was often the case, she was interrupted in her writing and finished over a period of days. As news of the battle of Perryville, Kentucky, reached southern Ohio, Mary Ann, her sisters and her mother were all anxious about the welfare of family and friends. Reports from the papers indicated that there were enormous losses on both sides, and Mary Ann finished her letter with questions about the battle. She anxiously awaited news from her husband regarding his health as well as that of her brother James and other friends.

Sergeant Montgomery was eager to provide details regarding the battle and attempted to answer some of Mary's questions regarding casualties.

Chattanooga, Tenn. Oct. 17, 1862
Dear wife. Today I was the happy recipient of a letter from you being date Oct. 6th. You can easily imagine with what pleasure I made myself master of its contents. I sincerely regret that our loved little one has had to suffer a severe illness but I am truly thankful that God has spared her to us and I hope that she may not be called on to suffer so again. Be careful of her Dear Mary for should I lose my darling Ella, half of my happiness in this world would be lost.

Dear Mary I have great cause to be thankful for the many blessings that has been meted out to me while others have been cut off in battle. I have witnessed death in almost every form. I have stood where it seemed impossible for man to stay and live but so it is a man may escape unhurt from the thickest of the fray and then he may think himself comparatively safe and the next moment he may be a corpse. But I need not dwell on the gloomy subject longer. God has been merciful to me and I am thankful and I humbly ask his kind protection in future for the sake of you and my darling child. Dear Mary I wrote yesterday so you see I have no news to write.

I can however answer your questions as regards Wm. Fullerton. He was killed instantly being shot through the head. He was left in the hands of the enemy and Capt Singer [John P. Singer had been promoted to captain of Company A upon the death of Captain Currie], we suppose is also in the hands of the enemy. We have not heard from him since the battle.

Record keeping was a problem during the Civil War and men were often listed as killed, when in fact, they were wounded or missing. Another problem arose from the fact that sometimes the occasional visitor to the regiment had traveled a great distance for a visit and had then decided to join the regiment in the field. One such individual was nineteen-year-old Sgt. William Fullerton, Company A, Thirty-third Ohio, of Wheelersburg, who was originally reported as one of the fatalities in the battle at Perryville, Kentucky. Apparently William Fullerton was wounded at Perryville, but recovered and eventually rejoined the regiment. Sergeant Fullerton was later killed at the battle of Chickamauga, Georgia, on September 20, 1863.

> When you write again tell me all of the particulars of the fire at neighbor John's [Kennedy] and tell me what the general opinion is as regards the author of all of the mischief that has been going on for the last few months. But for the want of time I shall be obliged to bid you a fond good bye until another time. Give my love to mother. My respects to all and accept my hearts warmest love for yourself and Ella. Now farewell. Mc Montgomery to his cherished wife Mary.

The regiment's commander, Col. Joshua Sill, had been promoted to brigadier general on July 16, 1862, and was given command of a division, and thus was not with the Thirty-third at Perryville. It was Col. Oscar F. Moore of Portsmouth, Ohio, who commanded the regiment in battle. Changes in command were often not of immediate concern to the foot soldier and thus were not mentioned in letters to family. That sort of news was gleaned from local news accounts. This was true also, of the news that Maj. Don Carlos Buell was removed from command after his failure to advance again the Confederate forces of Braxton Bragg. The *Portsmouth Times* carried news from Colonel Moore that the regiment had lost 118 men—25 men killed, 5 died later of their wounds, 70 were wounded or missing. The Montgomery family read the report with growing alarm. A few weeks later, McLain wrote to Mary Ann with more details of the fight.

October 26th 1862
Lebanon, Kentucky

Dear wife. I take the first opportunity after the receipt of your letter to answer it. The next day after I wrote to you at Louisville, we received marching orders and started in the direction of Taylorville [Kentucky], but we did not remain there but I will not give the details of the fatiguing march but come at once to the place where we stopped to some purpose.

On the night of the 7th we camped near Manville seven miles from

Perryville. We was on the road early next morning. We had not marched but a short distance before we heard the roar of artillery. Every mile the sound came nearer and clearer. About noon we came in sight of the combatants. We had one battery of artillery placed on a hill about half a mile from the rebel's battery and they gave shot for shot and shell for shell. But we did not remain inactive long. Our regiment was sent out on the left to prevent a surprise from that direction. It being woodland, our regt was formed in the edge of the woods with an open field on our right and a small cornfield on the left. Co. A and Co. F was sent out in advance some three hundred yards to reconnoiter.

We had not been there long before a regt. of cavalry [Col. John A. Wharton's cavalry brigade] made its appearance on our front and a regt of infantry on our left [Forty-first Georgia Infantry, Brig. Gen. George Maney's brigade]. We fired one round, killed their flag bearer and a few other of their men and then we retreated back to our regt., the rebels following close to our heels. The cavalry charged across the open field on our right, but we gave them such a warm reception that they charged the other way with much loss and in much confusion. By this time the infantry engaged us in numbers far superior to our own. We fought until nearly surrounded. We then fell back over the hill where we was relieved by the 24th Ill. We fought until dark hid the combatants from each other. The battle was a severe one and many brave man slept their last sleep on that bloody field, but I will omit details until a more pleasant day.

The snow is four inches deep that fell last night. We have no tents and it is cold now and I must quit by saying that James and me have both whole hides yet are both tolerable well at present. I wrote a letter and sent by Capt. Singer and told you that I had received the stamps you sent. After I sent that letter I had no opportunity to send letters. I am truly sorry that you are left alone. I would do almost anything but desert to get to be at home with you and my little pet. Mary you don't know how many sleepless hours I pass by the campfire thinking of you and my child. Now Mary write soon and send a few stamps and I will try and give you a letter for every one you send. I lost a part of them you sent on the battlefield. I lost my knapsack and blanket and I have had none since. Give my love to mother and all who may enquire. Write soon and direct to Lebanon Ky. Via. Louisville

33rd Rgt. McM to Mary

It was a solemn and frightening letter and Mary felt a profound sense of emptiness. She longed for some assurance that her husband would return to her unharmed. The loneliness seemed especially oppressive in the dreary winter months. Thoughts of her husband and brother without tents, sleeping exposed to the elements while she and Ella were warm and safe at home consumed her. It was also difficult to join in the festivities of the season with her mother and sisters as they planned a Thanksgiving meal that she would be unable to share with her husband. The sense of isolation was even more oppressive as she waited daily for the much anticipated mail hoping that it would bring word from him. But her hopes were dashed daily throughout the month of November as no letters arrived. When a letter finally arrived in December it revealed that McLain like his wife, was disappointed that he had not received mail from his loved one. Both were hurt and disappointed.

Nashville, December 8th, 1862
Dear wife. I seat myself to pen a few hurried lines to inform you of my whereabouts and enquire why you have not written. I wrote to you while at Lebanon and have waited patiently for an answer until I have come to the conclusion that my last letter has miscarried. I have received two letters from sister Abigail and one from brother Dell. I have answered them both and am looking for a return answer from them again. We are now camped near Nashville but we are under orders to be ready to march at a moments notice, so I have not time to add much more. When we get settled again I will write a long letter and give you a sketch of our travels since I wrote last, but my time is limited so you must excuse this short letter. Hoping to hear from you soon and praying that this may find you enjoying good health. I bid you goodbye. Kiss Ella for me and give my love to mother and all who may enquire after the welfare of your affectionate husband Mc Montgomery.

P.S. While at Lebanon I expressed ninety dollars home of James and myself and sent an order to George Flanders to draw the money for you to save you trouble. [George W. Flanders was a forty-two-year-old tanner from Portsmouth, Ohio] Fifty dollars belongs to James he sent the money this time that mother thought was lost. Write and let me know if you have got it.

Yet another Christmas passed and Sergeant Montgomery spent it on the field of battle rather than at home with his wife and daughter. Mary Ann responded to the much-repeated requests from family members to entertain them by playing favorite songs and carols on the piano. But despite the apparent gaiety of voices raised in song, her heart was heavy and the music brought her no joy.

On Monday, December 22, the regiment had moved from Gallatin, Tennessee, to Nashville where they remained until Friday, December 26. On that date they began to move toward Murfreesboro for yet another anticipated battle against Confederate general Braxton Bragg. The battle began on December 31 and continued for two more days. Local papers carried the news of the death of the regiment's former commander, Brig. Gen. Joshua W. Sill, who was killed on the morning of December 31 while commanding a brigade in the division of Sill's long time friend, Brig. Gen. Philip Sheridan.

# CHAPTER 6

# *January–July 1863*

## *Battle of Stones River, Tennessee*

Mary Ann had read local news reports of the number of casualties at the battle of Stones River, Murfreesboro, Tennessee. They described the battle fought between December 31, 1862, through January 2, 1863, and noted that it resulted in the highest percentage to that date of casualties on both sides. The Portsmouth paper reported that the Thirty-third being held in reserve, had been more fortunate than many other regiments, but still had suffered two men killed and forty-one wounded or missing. The paper also listed the names of the two men killed: Pvt. Charles Fetters, and Pvt. John M. Vanderman, both of Company B. Mary Ann was relieved that no men from Company A had been killed. She felt even greater relief upon receiving word from her husband that he had escaped injury.

In his letter McLain provided a brief account of the battle and promised to give more details later. He mentioned recent letters he had received from his brother Del Montgomery who was still recuperating in a hospital from the wound he had received at Corinth. He also mentioned receipt of a letter from brother Del's wife, Abigail.

Murfreesboro, Tenn. January 9, 1863

Dear Wife. I know you will be disappointed at the length of this letter but you must forgive me for not writing a letter this time. Circumstances will not admit. I wrote a short letter while at Edgefield and have waited for an answer with great impatience until it has become necessary for me to write again. I suppose you have heard of the battle of Murfreesboro and probably a better account of it than I can give so I will omit all particulars this time and give them in my next. I will only add this much—James and I was in the battle and through the goodness of God come off safe.

I have received two letters from sister Abigail and one from brother Dell since I heard from you. Dell was still in Mississippi. His health is not very good. One of sister Abby's letters I will send with this. It may perhaps be interesting [to] you now. My time is almost up and I will have to look for a stopping place, but if nothing happens I will write to you next Sunday and give you the details of the battle and such other news as I think will interest you. I want to hear from home so bad that I am almost froze. So please write to me, Dear Mary and don't fail to tell me all about my little pet. Mary I would give all most anything in the world to see you and Ella but as that is impossible I hope you will write soon and let me know how you get along. Give my love to mother and all the family not forgetting yourself. Kiss Ella for me and write soon and may the hand of a merciful God shield and protect you is the prayer of your neglectful but not forgetful husband McLain Montgomery to Mary Montgomery.

P.S. James sends his love to all and says he will write soon. I want you to give me George's address, his Co., his Capt's name, etc. Yours affectionately Mc.M.

Murfreesboro, Tenn. Jan. 17th 1863

Dear wife, a few days ago I wrote a few lines to you and promised to write again on Sunday, but I was on guard and had no opportunity to fulfill my promise. Since that time I have rec'd two letters from you. One containing four stamps, 3 for me and one for James. The other [contained] one sheet of paper, one envelope and one stamp. I was rejoiced to hear that you was well and Ella. I would forego all the honor I ever expect to gain in this war if I could only be at home and play with her for one day, but circumstances forbid my thinking of anything of the kind. But this I will try to do. I will write oftener and expect to hear from you more frequent.

In my last I promised to give you the particulars of the fight. I will do so as far as I am able. On Tuesday we moved up within 3 miles of Murfreesboro. Cannonading was kept up on our right with an occasional discharge of small arms throughout the day, but no general engagement took place.

On Wednesday morning we moved forward one mile, formed a line of battle. We did not remain long until we was called on to support the right. All the fighting being done in that direction. On we went on double quick for about half a mile, formed in line. During this time the rebels had driven our right back and left us nearly surrounded. We was then ordered back to support the centre. On came the rebels, flushed with victory, driving all before them. A Constant shower of shot and shell was poured in from us. From the direction of the town a heavy cavalry charge was made. At the same time, on our left, things began to look gloomy enough. Rebels to the right of us, to the left of us, in front of us and almost in the rear of us. It seemed impossible to escape. All at once the center became a line of fire. The artillery forming a semicircle kept up an incessant fire. The noise of the musketry much resembling a heavy windstorm. During this time we lay flat on the ground just in front of our artillery while it was pouring grape and canister shot and shell just far enough above our heads to miss us and making sad havoc in the rebels lines. For a while they stood it bravely and pushed forward a bit. It got too hot for them and the infantry fell back and the fighting was carried on by the artillery the balance of the day, except on the left of our center. There the battle raged until dark.

That night we stood picket on the field of battle the dead and wounded laying thick all around us. We suffered very much during the night from cold, no fire being allowed. The next day we was relieved long enough to eat a bite then came back on the field where we remained until Sunday evening without shelter or fire and scarcely anything [to] eat. The fighting stopped on Saturday evening. Monday we moved to Murfreesboro and here we are yet. I can't write as much as I intend this time but I will write next week again. Goodbye till then.

The following reference to George Montgomery's wife, Mary,

was an acknowledgement by Sergeant Montgomery that he had received the news that George and Mary were expecting their first child.

> Tell George's wife I wish her much joy. Kiss Ella for me and tell mother James is well and also tell her that I will try and prevail on him to write. I will send you $20 of confederate money just for to look at.
> McM. to Mary M

General Rosecrans, who had assumed command of the Army of the Cumberland after the battle of Perryville, received high praise from his superiors in Washington for his performance at Stones River. However, he failed to take aggressive action despite repeated urging from Gen. Henry W. Halleck and kept his troops idle at Murfreesboro for nearly six months following the battle.

## *Time on Their Hands: Home on their Minds*

Murfreesboro, Tenn. Jan. 25, 1863

Dear Wife, this is the third letter that I have written since the 1st of Jan., but I have received none from you of a later date than Dec. 23rd, yet I hope there is one on the way for me now. I have no news to write in particular at this time, but my time hangs heavily on my hands and I have little else to do than think of home and the loved ones that [I] long so much to see. Being a little better prepared to write than usual, I intend to commit to your care more of my thoughts than I have been in a habit of here to fore.

I frankly acknowledge that I [have] been neglectful but I will try and be more faithful in future. Here to fore my facility for writing has been very limited being the most of the time on the march and when not marching on picket or some other duty that made it inconvenient to write. Now it is different. We go on picket once in about 20 days and I go on camp guard in about 15 days so [you] see much of my time is my own, which time I pass in reading whatever comes in my way and that is but little, and in thinking of the happiness I could enjoy at home with you and Ella. Not a night passes that I do not lay awake thinking of you and my child wondering how my little pet looks since she has grown.

In her last letter Mary Ann had shared with her husband the difficulty and frustration she was experiencing in coping with their young daughter. Motherhood turned out to be more challenging than she had expected, especially how best to discipline the child. In Mary Ann's mind, truthfulness, was of utmost importance, but was a virtue, which little Ella had not yet mastered. Mary had exhausted her repertoire of disciplinary measures in her efforts to improve the child's behavior and looked forward to any helpful suggestions her husband might be able to make. McLain offered some advice to Mary regarding how best to deal with their young daughter. Bearing in mind that he had not seen his daughter since she was only a few months old, and that he clearly longed to be home, he had no point of reference as to what might or might not work with a young child. Nor could he understand why his wife seemed to have such difficulty in dealing with these little problems on the home front.

As she read the letter she was ashamed that her initial response was one of annoyance. How could he criticize her abilities as a mother? But, deep down, she realized that she had, after all, asked for his advice. She knew he loved them both and that his intent was to offer comfort, but his comments still carried a sting. She understood very well that she could not comprehend the trials her husband faced on the battlefield, but she suspected that her husband had absolutely no clue about the realities of dealing with a two year old. However, just then, her sister Cynthia's two daughters, raced through the house with their mother fast on their heels, yelling in a rage over a mess the two had just created in the kitchen. Here was an obvious proof that her sister's parental methods had yielded unsatisfactory results. Perhaps, she conceded, her husband might be right after all.

Mary you don't know how I love that child. I love wildly madly. If I could get hold of her I would be almost crazy with delight, but you must not think that I love you less since I have another to love. No, I love you more,

Dear Mary, because you are her mother and Mary whatever you do, watch over her and as she grows older, instill in her young mind the principles of truth. Talk to her as though she was capable of understanding. In this way she will understand the sooner and if I am spared to come home, nothing could please me better than to find my little girl obedient and truthful. Never promise her anything you don't intend to give her. Do not scold her, nor whip her, but if she does wrong, reprove her gently and without passion. She will soon understand you and obey you through love alone.. These rules may be hard to practice, but I am satisfied it is the best way. You will not have far to go to see the effects of the opposite treatment.

Now Mary, receive the assurance of my unchangeable love. Kiss Ella for me. Give my love to mother and my best respects to George's wife and then write to me your husband, Mc M. to Mary

James wrote to mother today. He is well.

Feb. 6th, 1863, Murfreesboro, Tenn.

Dear wife. Without waiting a reply from any of the several letters that I have posted for you, I take my pen to acknowledge the receipt of a letter through Wm. Fullerton, also the articles mentioned therein. You may rest assured they was thankfully received.

Young Sgt. William Fullerton, who had mistakenly been reported as killed at the Battle of Perryville, was, indeed, alive and well and had been granted a furlough after being wounded. As was often the case, friends and neighbors would request that a soldier returning to his regiment carry with him letters and supplies for men in the field. Fullerton had informed the good ladies of Wheelersburg of the need in the field for certain items. Socks were a particular priority since those supplied by the army or camp sutlers were, according to the men, too short and too thin to last anytime at all. In addition to articles of clothing, paper, envelopes and stamps were always in short supply and were welcomed by the men. Accordingly, over the long winter months, Mary Ann, her mother Nancy and sisters Cynthia and Sarah occupied much of their time in knitting items for McLain, James, and George.

In the brief paragraph below McLain acknowledged the receipt of the sad news that Mary's brother George and his wife Mary had lost their young daughter who was just twenty-four days old. The child,

Emma V. Montgomery, was buried in the Wheelersburg Cemetery.

I sincerely sympathize with George and his wife in the loss of their first born and such poor consolation as a soldier's sympathy can give is truly theirs.

While Mary Ann was only too happy to learn that her husband and his regiment had been relatively inactive since the battle at Stones River, she was sad that he seemed to be so homesick and depressed. She could not, however, avoid a feeling of great happiness that he missed her as much as she missed him.

Dear Mary, I am gloomy and despondent. My mind agrees very well with the stormy weather that has prevailed here for several days and perhaps the weather has something to do with my feelings. Perhaps it is the inactivity of camp life, but whatever it may be, do not let the knowledge of it give you any uneasiness. For let me assure you there is no visible cause for it, but this much I do know, one hour of your presence would dispel my gloom and make my poor heart glad indeed. But as such bliss is denied me, I will cherish each and every little gift from you as dearly as though they was priceless gems. Your letter(s) every one, are treasured up and are brought from their hiding places and read over and then carefully replaced. But Mary, let us hope for a reunion when we will never be separated again until we have long enjoyed the happiness we sought in each other's society.

But Mary Dear, I will leave a subject that awakens feelings of regret. I will now give you a short chapter of a soldiers life in active service. Early in the month of January, the weather was fine. We had done everything we could to do to our comfort. During our temporary stay at this place most of us might be seen eating our course meal when the assembly is sounded on the bugle. Just look at the magic there is in that sound. Everything is life and activity. The half finished meal is abandoned, guns is examined, cartridge boxes is hastily buckled on and in five minutes after the bugle sounded, the 33rd could be seen in line on their parade ground anxious to know what occasioned the alarm. The commanders of companies marched to the front to get their instructions. The order was brief and to the point. Have the men in marching order to move at a moments notice. One day's rations in haversack. Then commences a scene that is beyond description. A regiment getting ready to move on short notice.

We will pass over the preparations and listen to what is being said in camp: "I wonder what's up? Where are we going? How long will we be gone? Which way are we going? I wish they had waited until we finished dinner," were questions and remarks that were to be heard from every direction. Then starts a rumor in some part of the camp that our forage train is being attacked and by the time it has passed through the reg't. it has been changed and magnified until we hear that Bragg and his army is within six hours march of our camp. But conjectures and grapevine dispatches are cut short by the second sound of the bugle. Again we are in line. One blanket, gun and cartridge box and one day's rations fits us for the trip. Away we go and soon come up with the rear of the forage train that went out early in the morning. Then commences a host of questions: "Why don't you go ahead, what did you stop for, Is there any rebs out here?" Then comes the answers about as sensible as the questions. "Bragg's picket halted us." "We had no pass or have forgot the countersign or we go until we have passed our last picket post". Then every citizen is questioned and we get full as great a variety of stories from them as we would from the soldiers. One telling us that a few cavalry had been seen. The next would tell us that there was five or six regiments of infantry, as many reg'ts of cavalry and twelve or fifteen pieces of cannon. Perhaps the next would say there was none and had been none. So the time passes until dark. We are in a strange place knowing nothing about the country except the way to camp. And well we know we can't get there before tomorrow and we go through groves of cedar dark as Erebus, over logs, through mud and water, sometimes knee deep.

At last about an hour after dark and ten miles from camp we stop in an open field, well fenced with cedar rails. The house is near by and the numerous negro huts and many out buildings give signs of great wealth. But let us go back to the field and see what the boys is doing. Well, we find them preparing the evening meal. Some is carrying rails; some kindling a fire; some has gone to the barn after chickens. Some have come in with geese [and] others have gone to the smoke house to cut some meat for supper. Some prefer mutton and have killed a sheep. Well, I must see about my supper. I find my mess making a fire. I go for water and to save time I come back by the sweet potatoe hole to get a few for supper. When I get back there is a good fire and cooking commences. We boil our coffee water in our tin cups and make our coffee in the same. We sharpen sticks and stick a sweet potatoe on the end of it and hold it in a hot place to roast for we have no ashes yet. We fry our meat in the same way that we roast our potatoes. An hour and supper is over. We then go to bed. Two sleeping together laying on one blanket and covering with another. We sleep perhaps as sound as many others who have better beds. So the night passes and day comes again.

Let us look around and see where we are. We find ourselves on a plantation of many hundred acres of splendid farming land. Not a fence in sight. The rails were mostly burnt last night. We have some sweet potatoes left for breakfast. We make some more coffee in our tin cups and in an hour we are ready to leave: over one hundred wagons have been loaded with corn, hay and oats, leaving a farm without fences, a barn without fowls and an empty smoke house and some very sour faces behind. By noon we are in camp again and everything relapses into the monotony of camp life, but we never know when this same thing is to be enacted over again. We occasionally hear the report of cannon in the direction of Shelbyville, but we have got used to such noises and pay very little attention to it. But Mary, I am spinning my yarn too long. I must wind up. James wrote to mother a few days since and I will try to get him to write again. In this he sends his love to mother and all who may inquire after his welfare. Now Mary good bye. Kiss Ella for me and give my love to mother and George's family and all who claim my regards. Write soon for I am lonesome. Accept this from your absent but loving husband. Mc Montgomery to Mary.

P.S. Enclosed you will find a confederate P.O. Stamp of no value of course but you perhaps never saw one. Mc. M.

Murfreesboro, Feb. 14th 1863
Dear wife, today I rec'd a letter from you dated Jan. 21st and I find by it that you have not yet rec'd all of my letters. I have received the two letters that you mentioned and the stamps, also I answered both of them. I also answered the one you sent [by] Wm. Fullerton. I have nothing to write that would inter-

est you, but I suppose you will look for an answer and if the post office department does its share you will get it.

Enclosed in your letter I found a tress of Ella's hair and very proud I am of it too. Mary was it foolish for me to kiss it? If it was then I have acted foolishly for I kissed it many times. I shall keep it carefully although I do not need anything to remind of the little pet. Now Mary, I shall have to quit for want of something to write. It is night and it is raining and very dark. My tent leaks some and it is bad writing so I will close this for the morning mail and if it should be fortunate enough reach its destination. I hope it will find you enjoying all of the blessing of an ever indulgent providence. Give my love to mother and all of the friends and write soon. All is well. Your affectionate husband.
Mc. Montgomery to Mary

In his letter of February 19, McLain once again provided family news from Illinois, and acknowledged a letter from his sister, Albina and her husband, Alexander Hamilton Janes.

Murfreesboro, Feb. 19th, 1863
Dear Wife. I rec'd your letter dated (?) yesterday and take the first opportunity to answer it. I have nothing to tell that would interest you much, so if my letter is short, you must not complain and if it was not for gratifying your desire to know how I am I would not write for a while. In your letter you stated that you had rec'd 3 letters from me that was written in Jan. There must be one or two on the way yet for I wrote in two that I had rec'd your Lebanon and Nashville letters. In one of my letters I enclosed $20 in Confederate money. Of course it is of no use to you. I sent it just for curiosity. When you write again, let me know if you have rec'd it.

I rec'd a letter from my brother in law, A. H. Janes a few days ago. They were all well at that time. The letter bears the date of Feb. 5th. It states that Delorain is discharged from the service. His family lives in Amboy [Illinois] about 30 miles from Walnut where they used to live. Sister Albina sends her love to you and would be glad to open correspondence with you. I have not heard from Abigail nor Del for a long time except through James' letter.

Your letter stated that it was very cold at the time of writing. At the same time it was very warm here. Today we have no fire in the tent. It is comfortable enough without. It has been raining considerable for the last week and the waters is high. The cars runs from Nashville here. The mails are more regular. James is well. I am well and now for the way of something to write, I will quit. Kiss Ella for me and write often. Good bye, God Bless you is the prayer from your affectionate husband,
McLain Montgomery to Mary Montgomery

When Mary Ann opened the letter March 27, 1863, she was pleased to see that her husband was still in camp at Murfreesboro. But the most pleasant surprise of all was the photograph that fell out of the envelope when she opened it. It was a treasure like none other.

Murfreesboro, Tenn., in camp March 27th 1863
Dear wife. Since I wrote last nothing of importance has taken place to vary the regular routine of camp duty. I was in hopes that I would hear from you before this and now I hope there is a letter on the way for me now. If there is not, I hope you will start one very soon, but I well know that I'm remembered at home and I can wait your pleasure. In my last letter I gave you reason to hope that I would visit home this spring. I still think I will come but I don't expect I can get off before the first of June. But do not make any great calculations soon. I may not come at all, but I will come if possible.

Enclosed you find a likeness. Please tell me in your next if you recognize it or not. If you do not, I think I will keep you in the dark a while and I don't know whether that would be forward. Now for sixteen months hard service has changed the original sadly, yet I must acknowledge that the original is in better health than he has been for a year, with the exception of a plueralgia pain in the left cheek, there is nothing to complain of and as the spring advances that is less frequent.

The spring is very backward here to what it was a year ago. The peach trees is in full bloom and the early forest trees is getting green yet the nights are cool. Sometimes frost. Today is warm and showery corresponding very well with our April weather although the season for farmers to sow that they may reap is here, nothing in the agriculture line is doing. The country around here is as well outfitted as to farming as any I ever saw, yet instead of the plough in the field, you can picture to yourself bodies of around thousands broad fields of two and three hundred acres are used only for drill ground for the Union legions.

From appearances our General expects an attack on this place. At least they are preparing for such an event. We are daily fortifying and this is likely to become one of the strongest military posts in the Southwest and if we have to fight Bragg's army again, I hope he comes here to us. But if he don't come, I have some hopes of being left here. General [Lovell H.] Rousseau has come back and has taken command of his old division again and it is thought he will be left here. But I must begin to look for a stopping place.

The bugle sounded for dress parade just now and I had to quit, but on account of the weather we was recalled, so I begin again. I wish Mary, you could see us here as we are. The reg't is in general good health, in fine spirit, and ready to do anything to serve our country. We have new colors of which we are very proud. Chaplin Hills and Stone River is inscribed on them, sighting us back to our hardships and trials, our laurels is richly earned and we have a right to be proud of them. A few weeks ago I sent you a picture of the battle of Stone River. If it has reached you, you can see the position of the 33rd Reg't. On the right of the turnpike leading to Murfreesboro, laying flat on the ground where we lay for four weary days and nightly half frozen and most starved. So you can judge whether we deserve the honor that is given us or not. But it is getting dark and after asking you to kiss Ella for me and biding you a fond good bye, I close hoping to hear from you soon.
Mc M. to Mary

P.S. James is well and J.C. Hungerford [James C. Hungerford, Sergeant, Company E] requests you to say to his folks that he is well.
Mc. M.

As usual, the mail was unreliable. It was not unusual for letters to arrive weeks after they had been sent and of course, sometimes they were lost in transit. This caused much distress to both Mary and to her husband and they each urged the other to be more diligent in their letter writing. Although Mary was pleased that her husband shared with her news he received from his siblings in Illinois, it sometimes saddened her that he seemed more excited about their letters than he did about hers.

April 6, 1863, Murfreesboro, Tenn.
Dear Wife. Yesterday I had the pleasure of reading your kind letter bearing date March 27th so you will see by referring to the date of this that I am not slow to answer not with standing my western correspondence. It is unkind of you Dear Mary to accuse me of preferring other correspondence to that of yours. It is true that I read eagerly and with great pleasure every letter from my brothers and sisters and answer them cheerfully, yet I find more true pleasure in one letter from my dear wife, than I do in all of the others put together. And I am sure you did not mean what you said about my not wanting to hear from you. Yes, Mary, your letters are most eagerly looked for and first answered of all of the letters I get, but you know this before. While speaking of letters, I will mention one I sent to you a few days ago. It contained a likeness but as you did not recognize the lock of hair that I sent I will leave you to guess whose likeness it is. The hair was mine.

In an earlier letter dated February 19, from Murfreesboro, McLain had included information he had received from his brother-in-law Alexander Hamilton Janes. The letter contained news of the February 9 marriage of McLain's fifteen-year-old niece, Lorain McNitt. She was the daughter of McLain's sister Francina and Elijah McNitt. Mary Ann was both surprised and shocked at the news. It wasn't so much the fact that the girl was only fifteen, but rather that she had married forty-eight-year-old widower, Oliver Hazard Hastings. Hastings was the father of Abigail Hastings, wife of McLain's brother Del. Mary could not imagine how the McNitt's had allowed this to happen. What on earth could the new couple possibly have in common?

In your letter you expressed some surprise at the Illinois wedding that I spoke of. I am sure no one could be [more] astonished than I was. I remembered the bride only as a little girl that I used to carry in my arms and Hastings, I knew as an old widower. One that I thought would never marry again. But strange things happen and that is one of them, but the mail will leave soon and if I am in time with this I must wind up.

The weather is fine, rather warm to be comfortable At present I am not very well, but I don't think any thing serious is the matter. James is well. He is out with the reg't working on the fortifications. He got a letter from home yesterday, but I did not see it. The day before I received a letter from A. P. Osborn [Arthur P. Osborn, resident of Wheelersburg] but I must finish. I want you to kiss Ella for me and write often and never fear of me getting tired of answering you letters. Now, Mary, good bye, God bless you and my darling Ella.
Ever yours Mc to Mary

P.S. Your last letter was directed to the 3rd Division, 9th Brigade that once was right but there have been changes made so it is different now. We are now the 1st Division and the 1st brigade in the 14th Army Corps in the Department of the Cumberland, but it is not necessary to put all of the above on a letter.. 33rd O.V.I., U.S.A. Murfreesboro, Tenn. Co. A.

April 13, 1863, Murfreesboro, Tenn.
Dear Wife. I have time for only a few words. In a few days I can write at more length. I rec'd yours of April 6th and was rejoiced to hear that you and Ella was well. Today I will send 35 Dollars by L. Young [thirty-three-year-old Lewis Young was a carpenter from Green Township, Adams County, Ohio, who was visiting the camp] deeming it as safe as any other way I could send. In deed it is the only way I can send it except by mail. I could send more but I do not like to trust it all at once. Besides I hope I may be able to come myself after a while, but I have no time to write more as I will have to go on inspection.
From your affectionate husband
Mc. Montgomery to Mary Montgomery
Kiss Ella. Good bye, God Bless you

# CHAPTER 7

# Women at Home and Those at the Front

As always, Mary Ann couldn't take the time to sit down before opening the latest letter, but eagerly tore open the envelope dated April 19, 1863. As she began to read, she smiled to herself at her husband's apparent embarrassment over his sister Albina's teasing about his boastful claims regarding little Ella's beauty. It was true that she had, with a mother's pride, written to their Illinois kin that Ella was the spitting image of her father. In Mary's eyes the two loves of her life were indeed beautiful, and she knew that Albina meant no disrespect. But the sister clearly enjoyed some playful kidding at her younger brother's expense.

In camp at Murfreesboro, Tenn. April 19th, 1863
Confidential Private
Dear wife. Today I received yours of the 11th and as it is Sunday and I have plenty of time to answer it and if I had anything to write about I would write you a long letter, but one day is so much like another here and so little change in our way of living that I would have to be the possessor of a very fertile imagination to find material for a long letter. But you are generous enough to excuse me for writing one short letter, You said you had got that

picture that I sent but you did not say whether Mother had got hers that James sent or not, nor did you say what you thought of it.

Today I wrote to sister Albina. I wrote her a long letter. Told her all about my little Ella. I told her that Ella was the best looking Montgomery that I ever saw. About that time I got your letter and told her what you said—Ella looking like me. I expect she will think I have exalted ideas of my good looks. You see that all comes of your notions of beauty. Now I know Ella is pretty and you say she looks like me and Albina knows that I am anything else but good looking. But oh Mary, I would give anything in the world for just one kiss from that little pet, but Mary for all of my love for Ella you are uppermost in my mind. When I wake in the morning you are scarce ever absent from my mind. Through the day and at night I lay down only to dream of you and home and such pleasant dreams. I [am] so anxious for the cursed rebellion to end so that I may be permitted to taste the sweets of home that I know awaits me. I can imagine no joy so great as that of pulling you to my bosom and tasting the sweet warm kiss from lips that I know has ever been true to me.

Mary Dearest, I am getting foolish. I think and if I go on at this rate, I am afraid you will think so too. Maybe I am getting old and childish, but that can't be either for I am hale and hearty and feel better than I ever have felt since I left home. I was very glad to hear that you and Ella was well and I hope that God will be merciful, shield you both from harm and permit me to live to come back to you. A few days since I wrote to you and enclosed thirty-five dollars and entrusted the same to the care of Lewis Young who was going to Portsmouth. I expect you will receive it before you get this. I did not write much in that letter because I had not time and now I have plenty of time and nothing to tell you that would interest you. Particularly we have not been out of sight of our tents for a month.

## Private—Confidential

Yes, Mary, I have a little piece of news to tell you that is out of the course of common events entirely. A night or two since on picket, a Sergeant of one of our volunteer regiments gave birth to a child, but I have not learned whether the little stranger is a boy or girl as the sergeant has been in the service over a year it is reasonable to suppose that the little pledge of love was gotten in true military style. It had ought to be a hero and very fond of martial music, but Mary, you need not fear for old Sergt Montgomery.

But Mary, here is marching orders, two days rations in haversack and be ready to move at a moments notice. So one imaginary kiss for you and Ella and then good bye.
Yours in true love as ever.
Mc. to Mary. Direct as before.

Mary Ann had heard rumors about the large numbers of women who gathered around military camps supposedly as cooks and laundresses, but who were, in reality prostitutes. But this business about women masquerading as men and serving in their regiments was new. She felt confident in her husband's fidelity, but couldn't help being upset. He had warned her that the information was "private and confidential," but she had to share it with her mother and sisters. She also tried to discreetly inquire of other soldiers' wives in the area if they had heard anything about these women.

## Soiled Doves and Horizontal Refreshments

The incident described by Sergeant Montgomery so provoked Gen. William Starke Rosecrans, that he described the event as "a flagrant outrage" and "a violation of all military law." Rosecrans, upon learning of the situation, ordered his aide-de-camp, Frank J. Boyd to send the following telegram to Maj. Gen. Alexander McD. McCook who was in command of the Twentieth Army Corps:

(April 17, 1863)
General. The general commanding me to call your attention to a flagrant outrage committed in your command: a person having been admitted inside your lines without a pass and in violation of orders. The case is one which calls for your personal attention, and the general commanding directs that you deal with the offending party or parties according to law.

The medical director reports that an orderly sergeant in B.G [Richard W.] Johnson's division was today delivered of a baby— which is in violation of all military law and of the army regulations. No such case has been known since the days of Jupiter. You will apply the proper punishment in this case and a remedy to prevent a repetition of the act.

As with all situations where families are separated for long periods of time, war, with its perpetual threat of impending death or mutilation, produces, perhaps, the most profound effect on the human psyche. Behaviors that would have been unthinkable at home midst the moral constraints of society somehow seemed more reasonable, unavoidable or even normal near the battlefield.

There are documented cases of women who disguised themselves as men, adopted male names and served in the Civil War for both the Union and the Confederacy. Although the numbers are relatively small, various estimates range from four hundred to one thousand, the discovery of the women's true identity always resulted in their removal from the army. Some had enlisted to be by the side of their husbands and brothers or lovers. Some were motivated by true patriotism and a desire to serve their country in the nontraditional male role despite the prevailing social restrictions. Some were wounded in battle and some were taken captive and suffered in prison camps before their true identity was discovered. There were others, however, who adopted the gender subterfuge as a cover for their true motives and profession, i.e. prostitution. Their identity, more often than not, was discovered as the result of their behaviors.

As was usual in cases in which women had been masquerading as soldiers, the army took great pains to cover up the situation. Of course, the men often were eager to share the news with folks at home. One soldier, unlike Sergeant Montgomery who warned Mary that the information was secret, wrote a letter to his local newspaper and included in his account the news that the woman had been in the war for twenty months and that no one had suspected her of being a man. The editor of the newspaper found this to be amusing and suggested that the baby's father must have had a pretty strong suspicion.

The large numbers of women who congregated around men at army camps had quickly learned that they earned far more for their sexual skills than for their ability to wash clothes or cook up a tasty meal. These "soiled doves" as they were sometimes called offered a satisfying, but temporary sexual diversion to the lonely soldier. Unfortunately these brief episodes of horizontal refreshment proved to levy a much steeper cost than the soldier expected since the women, more often than not, distributed a variety of venereal diseases that lasted far longer than the brief encounter.

*Prostitute*
<small>Courtesy of Elizabeth Ann Topping</small>

It had been several weeks since Mary Ann had received a letter from her husband and during those times, she always worried that he might have suffered some illness or have been wounded, or that he might have succumbed to the wiles of a soiled dove. She was surprised when her husband confided little pieces of gossip, for it seemed so uncharacteristic of him. But she was glad for any and all news that he wanted to share, and in some ways, the fact that he shared the information with her surely meant that he would never engage in such activity. It was with great relief that she opened his letter dated May 8.

Murfreesboro, Tenn. May 8th 1863
Dear Mary. I received your letter dated Apr. 27 on May the 3rd and my excuse for not answering it sooner is the weather has been so wet and cold I could not write with any comfort. So I kept putting it off until I was ashamed to wait longer and now I have no news to give you but still I take pleasure in writing to you even if I had nothing to say only that I am well and I can hardly say that this time the bad weather has brought on an attack of neuralgia that gives me great pain. But I have no doubt but it will disappear as soon as the weather settles. I have been subject to it for the last six months and fair weather always dispels it. So you see there is

no cause for any uneasiness. James is in good health and says to send a piece of his whiskers to mother [which] would be impossible as he is smooth shaven. But I will try and prevail on him [to] send a lock of his hair the next time he writes.

## A Little Gossip

Now Mary I have some private gossip to write. It is intended for your eye only. I don't know whether I had ought to tell you or not, but it is only to let you see the effect of army influence on some people. W.B. McNeal on coming into the service was a church member and two years in army has had the following effect on him. He is now a habitual swearer, frequently gets drunk and last of all and worst of all, he is now suffering from a disease that, I blush to mention, you will perhaps understand what it is when I tell you that he gave a woman 5 dollars for it in Nashville. And even under these circumstances, he is trying to get a leave of absence to come home. He would be in a fine fix to visit his wife. Don't you think he would? But this is none of my business and I doubt if I have done right in telling you. All I have to do is to behave myself and with God's help, I will try, and have no fear about that, I will succeed. Now, Mary, the above little story you will never mention, I know, but I will change the subject.

General Rosecrans's decision to keep his men encamped for nearly six months and his unwillingness to move aggressively against Bragg's Confederate troops, not only frustrated his superior officers, but also exacerbated the problem of the ever increasing numbers of prostitutes in Nashville, which was just thirty-one miles from Murfreesboro. By 1863 there was considerable concern regarding the significant increase in the number of cases of venereal disease, with estimates indicating that over the course of the war one in eleven Union soldiers was infected with either syphilis or gonorrhea.

The problem became so severe, that in July of 1863, the U.S. government rounded up prostitutes in Nashville, and put them on the steamer *Idahoe*, with orders to the captain of the vessel to take his cargo up stream. The captain first docked at Louisville, Kentucky, where the city officials refused to allow the female travelers to disembark. The captain, now stuck with his unwelcome cargo, next steamed further north to Cincinnati, Ohio, where he was once again refused permission to unload his passengers. Finally, after two more unsuccessful stops at other Kentucky riverport towns, the captain returned to Nashville. It was after this failed attempt to rid the city of these instruments of venereal disease, that Lt. Col. George Spalding, Union provost marshal, ordered that prostitutes be licensed following a medical exam to ensure that they were free of disease. The army later instituted a similar program in Memphis.

To be fair to the subject of the gossip, it should be noted that 1st Lt. Walter B. McNeal, Company A, formerly a flat boatman on the Ohio River, had enlisted in the Thirty-third Ohio at age twenty-six. It was his experience on the river that resulted in his being selected to command one of two fleets of boats on the night of Monday, October 26, 1863, at Chattanooga, Tennessee. Brig. Gen. William "Baldy" Smith, Grant's chief engineer had assigned the men in command of the boats to transport fifteen hundred men around Moccasin Bend in the Tennessee River under cover of darkness. Their goal was to reopen the river to enable Union forces to deliver much needed supplies and troops to the beleaguered troops at Chattanooga. In that operation, Lieutenant McNeal handled himself and the men under him with great efficiency and received high praise from his superiors. Apparently, however, Lieutenant McNeal had become weary of army life, or perhaps others had relayed word of his indiscretions to the folks at home. His reasons are unknown, but he resigned his commission and left the regiment in December of 1863.

## The Home Front

Although time and worry weighed heavily upon the adults at home, one routine that lifted everyone's spirits, especially those of the children, was the ritual of the Saturday night bath. Mary Ann's older sister, Cynthia, was the chief organizer and guiding force behind this event. Chairs for each child were drawn up in a semicircle around the fire as water was heated and poured into the waiting tub. Draped over the back of each chair were the nightclothes for each of the children and on the seat, was a carefully folded towel. One by one they each took their turn in the bath water and after a thorough scrubbing at the hands of their mothers, they were dried off, dressed in their bedtime clothes and returned to their assigned chair to await the completion of the baths. Once those were finished, Aunt Cynthia used the bath water to scrub the floor around the fireplace. Following the completion of this task and the drying of the floor, she tossed kernels of corn into the still smoldering fireplace and as the popped kernels exploded onto the freshly scrubbed floor, the children scrambled from their chairs to retrieve the delectable morsels. Once the popped corn had been consumed, the children enjoyed some warm milk and were entertained with family stories until one by one their sleepy eyes meant that it was time for bed. The routine yielded a cherished memory for them all, but it could not completely erase adult tensions.

Mary Ann tried hard to avoid worrying her husband about petty issues that arose at home. At the beginning of the war, her father, William Montgomery, was often away from home for months when his trips downriver to transport crops extended into lengthy, unexplained absences. More recently, the family had become concerned about the declining physical and mental state of the sixty-eight-year old farmer. Mary Ann, her mother, Nancy, and her brother George's wife, Mary, did their best to maintain the household and farm. But things had become strained between Mary Ann and her sister-in-law after the death of little Eva. Mary understood how devastating the loss of a child would be and felt deep empathy for the pain the young mother was experiencing. But it was upsetting that the grieving mother so deeply resented her own little Ella. At times, it seemed that she wished harm to her and her daughter. When she had tried to share her concerns with her sisters, Sarah and Cynthia, they were unsympathetic to her complaints and even suggested that it was she who was at fault for not being more understanding with their sister-in-law.

> There is some little enquiries about home that I wish to make. In the first place it has been a long time since you said a word about

George's wife. Does she still live with you and mother or not? And there is Sarah and Jose. You never tell me whether you ever hear of them or not and Jesse's folks. You never say a word about them. Now when you write again please write me all the news you can think of.

In your letter you told me I must not make fun of you for calling our little pet handsome. Pshaw, Mary. I did not intend to make sport of you. I was only laughing at the idea of me being good looking. You know you said she looked like me but I will not dispute with you about her looks for when I last saw her I thought she was the prettiest little brat if ever saw. But you see my paper is nearly full so I must quit by sending my love to Mother and all that are entitled to it and my respects to everyone that deserves them and very many kisses to Ella and my undivided love to you. From your true and faithful husband.
Mc Montgomery to Mary Montgomery.
Good Bye. God bless you.

About a week later, Sergeant Montgomery was surprised but pleased to receive a letter from his twenty-year-old niece, Adaline Janes, oldest daughter of his sister Albina. Adaline was full of news about family in Illinois and clearly enjoyed the opportunity to share it with her uncle.

May 9th 1863
Greenville

Dear Uncle,

I do feel a little ashamed of not writing to you before, but I thought that I would pay you up for not writing to me for so long. But I did not intend to be quite so long about it, but if you will forgive me this time, I will try and do better in the future. And I know you will for you have a kind forgiving nature and then I forgave you, Uncle Mc. For not writing to me.

Mother received a letter from you yesterday and she wanted me to answer it for her. Now Uncle Mc. I must answer it in my own way for I am a favor excuse to write a letter for anyone else. The other time I wrote to you I got a small lecture for writing more for myself than I did for Mother. But I am a poor letter writer at best for I have had no correspondence lately and I have got so that I can't write.

Uncle Dell's folks have moved down in the swamp near Green River. They were here yesterday and Aunt Abby scolded about your not writing to her. She said that she had written to you last and had looked for a letter from you a long time, but had looked in vane. Uncle Dell has got a nice place down there in the edge of the timber. It would be rather lonesome to some to live away off there alone, but it would not be lonesome for me. No, I should like to live in such a place away from the cares and temptations of the world. But no more of this or you will perhaps think that I am aiming to be a little romantic which is not the case.

Uncle Newton was initiated into the Good Templars Lodge last week. I have not seen him since last lodge night and he was well and the rest of the folks. Uncle John's folks are all well and Uncle Elijah's were well the last time we heard from them. I believe that is all that I should speak of in particular so I will write a little for Mother. She has just been in the room where I am writing to see what I had written, but I did not read it to her, for I never like to have anyone read my letters but the one I am writing to. She wants I should tell you that she wants you to send your picture to her. She was afraid that I would want you to send it to me and she would not get it for she well knew that I would get it if I could. But as much as I should like to have it, if you will send it to her, I will try and send you hers and mine for she wants to see you so bad. She told me to tell you that if you did have a smart baby that she did not believe that it was any smarter [than] our little Byron. He is one of the prettiest and smartest and most mischievous little fellows that you ever saw. He is almost sixteen months old and can say almost everything. But I suppose that your baby is just as smart as he is, but you and Mother likes to brag a little. I suppose that is natural. You know she would like to see your wife and baby and so would I. You must tell Aunt Mary to write to us. I should like to hear from here very much.

Mother's hair is almost as gray as her mothers was when she died. But I cannot see that she looks any older than she did when you went away. With the exception of her hair, she has been fleshier this winter and spring than she has years before and father's health has been better than usual. This winter he has been taking Golden ointment for the asthma and it appears to help him.

Francis has got your old fiddle yet and speaks about your coming back almost every day to play on it. Newton has not learned to play on it yet much for he has not got the patience to learn. He has got to be almost as tall as father and is a great help to him for he is a good boy and does all he can. We have a good spring here. The weather is warm and the most of the farmers have got their corn planted. Father finished planting last Saturday. I helped father plant his corn and then planted corn for Mr. Seger for 50 cts. a day. Don't you think that I am quite a nice little boy to be out in the cornfield planting corn.

In the following, Adaline reported on the welfare and activities of her younger sister, Francina Janes, wife of James Burke. Thirty-two-year-old James had enlisted as a corporal in Company H of the Ninety-ninth Illinois Volunteer Infantry on August 8, 1862. His expectations of a confrontation with Confederate forces at Vicksburg were well founded for on May 18, 1863, Gen. Ulysses S. Grant and his Army of Tennessee began their assault on Vicksburg, Mississippi. The campaign raged on until July 4, when Union forces secured the surrender of the garrison. This successfully gave command of the Mississippi River to Federal forces for the remainder of the war.

> Francina Burke is well and so are her children. Jim is down almost to Vicksburg. He was well the last Francina heard from him and expecting a fight with the rebels pretty soon. But I must close for this time. Hoping to hear from you as soon as possible and I will try and be more punctual in writing after this. Give my love to Aunt Mary when you write to her again and tell her to kiss little Ella for me. Tell her that I should like to have her write to me. Don't forget to send your picture Uncle Mc. And write soon. I will have father write if I can. Good Bye.

> Yours truly,
> Adaline E. Janes

> May 17th, 1863, Murfreesboro, Tenn.
> Dear wife. I have written since I received a letter from you but I expect there is a letter on the way for me now. At least I hope so. A few days since I received a letter from Adaline Janes. It is the first I have got from Illinois for some time. I will not write what she said but send her letter and let you read it yourself.

Yesterday James received a letter from mother stating that you was all well. I was very glad to hear that father was steadier in his habits and I hope he will continue to live so the remainder of his life. I will try and get James to write to him. I would write to him myself if I thought it would do any good. If you think it will, I will write.

I received a letter from my friend Osborn not long since. He gave me all of the Wheelersburg news and he likewise told me that you and Ella was well. Now, Mary, I have nothing more to write at present that would interest you so I will close. Give my love to George's folks. Write if you hear anything from George. Give my love to mother and father and kiss Ella for me and save good kisses for me when I come. Mary, very near two thirds of my time is put in and I still have some hopes of coming home between this and winter. Good bye Dearest Mary. Write often and remember yours ever true, Mc Montgomery to Mary Montgomery

# CHAPTER 8

# June–December
# 1863

Murfreesboro, Tenn., June 5th 1863

Dear wife. A few days since I rec'd a letter from you and it was welcomed with pleasure as it bore tiding of the good health of you and my darling pet, but as I had a letter on the road for you already and there being nothing new to write about, I have delayed answering it longer than I usually do. But I do not intend to give you cause to complain of neglect. You shall receive a letter from me as often as once a week as long as the mails will carry them.

For the last day or two there has been considerable excitement. Orders came for us to be ready to march at a moment's notice and yesterday, heavy cannonading was heard in our front during the most of the day and last night. Eighty of our wounded was brought in and from what I can learn, there was considerable of a battle fought, but today all is quiet and there is as little prospect of our leaving now as there was a week ago.

## Crime and Punishment

In the following passage Sergeant Montgomery shared with Mary an incident in which martial law was carried out swiftly and in the presence of soldiers in the area. It also provides a prime example that both

Union and Confederate officers cooperated in the administration of justice toward common criminals. The brutality of the man's crime clearly had a profound effect on the men. This was the first of several incidents that Montgomery and his fellow soldiers would witness, including the execution of one of their own for desertion.

This afternoon I witnessed the execution of a murderer. He was a rebel. His name was Wm. Selkirk. He was hung for the murder of an old man by the name of Oustenhaus. The old man was most brutally murdered, his ears being cut off and his tongue being cut out before he was killed. Since the execution, I have learned that General Bragg of the rebel army has one of Selkirk's confederates for the same crime and also that he sent a message to General Rosecrans requesting him to hang Selkirk. There was at least ten thousand persons present to witness his death. After he arrived at the gallows, he was baptized. Then his sentence was read and after that he was allowed five minutes to be occupied in any way he chose. About half of that time was spent in silent prayer. The remainder was taken in asserting his innocence and bidding farewell to his friends which were very few. The murdered man's daughter was present to see him die. She exhibited much vindictiveness. She even requested the privilege of tying the rope around his neck. Of course it was denied her. But I have taken up too much of my room with this sad story already. I will drop it.

Now Dear Mary, tell me how you and Ella is getting along. Does she learn to talk any? Can she ask about her papa? Is she as pretty as ever? Does she give you much trouble? Now Mary, give her twenty kisses and tell her I sent them. Write often. Give my love to father and mother and my respects to neighbor John and all who may inquire. Yours loving and true.
Mc M. to Mary.

It is impossible to know the tone of Mary's letter to which Sergeant Montgomery responded on June 9. However, whether her intent was to complain about the heavy workload she was experiencing at home, i.e., hoeing corn in the field: or whether she was merely relating to him her everyday activities which she must have felt seemed insignificant to those of her soldier husband.

Sergeant Montgomery sympathized, briefly, with the fact that she had to work in the field and reassured her that he would much prefer to be at home to do the work himself. He did not, however, hesitate to remind her that his duty was essential to the welfare of his country. That thought is punctuated with reference to the fact that his help was needed to protect his "country's flag" midst the "black clouds of war." This was a powerful image to put things into perspective for Mary.

It is apparent that Mary was hoping that her husband might be able to obtain leave for a visit home. She had pointed out to him that his nephew, 1st Lt. Homer Montgomery, Company A, Thirty-ninth Ohio, was back home in Scioto County on a furlough. Sergeant Montgomery felt there was little chance of that in the immediate future.

Murfreesboro, Tenn, June 9, 1863
Dear Wife. Yesterday I received a welcome message from you bearing the welcome intelligence of the good health of those I love and I can return to you the assurance of my good health. You stated that you had been out hoeing corn. Mary, I am sorry you have to go to the field to work and I look forward to the time when I can do the work in the field for you. At present my distracted country needs my help and I do not regret that I have separated myself from those that I love to lend a helping hand to protect my country's flag, but I think light is breaking through the black clouds of war and I trust our nation will soon rise above her troubles and then I look forward to a life of happiness with you and my dear little Ella. That will repay me for all the hardships that I have had to endure.

You said Homer Montgomery was at home on furlough. The way things stand here at present, it would be useless to ask for one but if Grant succeeds in taking Vicksburg, the chances will be better. But at present we are expected to watch Bragg, but if we meet with no bad luck, I think this fall will give us a sight of our friends. But it is near mail time and as I have a letter on the road for you that was written before I received your last, I will close. Give my love to mother and father. Tell them James is well. Kiss Ella for me and write often to your true and faithful husband.
Mc. Montgomery
Mary Montgomery

The health and welfare of Mary's younger brother James was of concern to his sisters and to his mother. It seems that James was none too fond of letter writing and needed perpetual prodding for him to undertake the process.

Murfreesboro, Tenn., June 21st 1863

Dear Wife. Yesterday I received yours of the 15th. The first I have heard from you for some time. I am rejoiced to hear that you are well, but I am grieved to learn that Ella is unwell and I hope you will write as often as you possible can and let me know how she gets along for I am very anxious to hear from her again as soon as possible. Tell Mother that I said nothing about James before because he was writing a letter for himself the same time. But I learned afterwards that he did not send his letter. He is writing again today, but for fear he does not finish his letter, I will just say he is well and sends his love and respects to all. You said that George wrote home that he would write to me. I have heard nothing from him yet. I wrote to him about the time that I wrote to you last. A few days since, I received two letters from Ills. One was from my brother Dell, and the other was from sister Abigail. They was all well.

Now I suppose you want to know what we are doing down here in Dixie. Everything has been quiet here for a long time. This morning, however, there is talk about marching and several cannon has been heard in the direction of Nashville. Last Thursday, there was two men hung here and yesterday our division was called to witness the death of a deserter. He was shot. The scene was solemn and imposing. The division was formed in a double hollow squared and the doomed man accompanied by the guard was marched around the square. His pall bearers followed him with his coffin. The brass band led the procession playing the death march. After passing around the entire square the[y] marched to the center. After a short prayer by the chaplain, he knelt by his coffin and in that position awaited the word that would end his career on earth. He had not long to wait. Eighteen muskets was fired at him and he died without a struggle.

Now dear Mary, I will have to bid you good bye for the present. Write soon and let me hear from Ella. Kiss her for me. Give my love to mother. My respects to all.

Yours, loving and true                    McMontgomery—Mary

## Smuggling in Memphis

Mary Ann's brother, shy, reserved George, found it impossible to discuss with his mother or sister anything that was in the least sexually suggestive. But some news was just too unusual to keep to himself and after dispensing with details of his duty in Memphis, Tennessee, he was eager to share the particulars of one of his new responsibilities with McLain.

> Camp of the 39th Ohio, Memphis June 24th 1863
> Dear cousin.
> Your welcome letter of the (?) came to hand in due time finding me in good health. We are still at Memphis and will stay here this summer, I think. We have pretty heavy guard duty to perform but that is not like marching. We have the nicest camp about Memphis, and the health of the regiment is good. There has [been] three cases of small pox, but they are all about well again. It has been pretty warm for awhile past and today it has been raining all day hard, and from appearance it will rain for a day or two as it generally does here.
>
> There is no very cheering news for a day or two past. Grant is progressing slowly confident of success all along. We hear that Joe Johns[t]on is massing a pretty large force in his rear but we have no fears for Grant's safety. We believe that Grant can whip him without raising the Siege of Vicksburg. We have seen many of the sick, wounded and prisoners from Stuart's Army. They are all confident of success and worship General Grant.

Despite the fact that Pvt. George Montgomery was clearly eager to tell his brother-in-law about the following episode, he appeared to be somewhat embarrassed about the duties he was required to do. In particular, it was the duty to search the numerous female smugglers in Memphis, which provoked his embarrassment.

The city of Memphis, Tennessee, had been surrendered to Union forces in June of 1862 and remained under Union control throughout the rest of the war. The citizens of that city, however, remained loyal to the Confederate cause. A major problem for the Union troops was the great number of women who congregated around the occupying forces. The majority were prostitutes but some were smugglers. The

*Memphis Prostitute*
PHOTO COURTESY OF ELIZABETH ANN TOPPING

Yankees viewed them as amusing entertainment, but considered them all to be completely lacking in morals. Their Confederate counterparts, however, praised them as loyal daughters of the South who were determined to "do all in their power to aid the Confederacy." They extolled the virtue of these women who were willing to "smuggle through the lines salt, medicine, clothing and other indispensables for their families in the Southern Army."

Whatever the true motivation of these women in Memphis, to farm boys from southern Ohio, proper ladies did not lift their skirts in public for any reason. As a result of the diligence of Union troops, there were a number of men and women who were arrested for smuggling and who were taken to Irving Block Prison, which had originally been used to house Yankee soldiers, but later was converted to a Confederate hospital. But upon the occupation of Memphis by Union troops in 1862 it was converted to a prison to hold Confederate prisoners of war. Southern publications loudly complained that it also held "ladies from fine families." The prison was eventually ordered closed by President Lincoln in 1865.

Well, Mc we have some amusing times here while on Grand Guard. There has been smuggling carried on here pretty extensively. Well, we have to examine every one that passes out. Well, there is a large population here of the fair sex. They are the ones that are doing the most of it. Well, our boys are pretty glad to see them. Sometimes they find one with medicines concealed about their person. They caught one with a small sack of quinine tied to her thigh. She was escorted to the Irving Block Prison. There has been a great many sent South from here. All that will not take the oath of allegiance to the United States are sent beyond our lines by order of General Hurlburt.

I suppose you have heard before this that our Lodge at the Burg [Wheelersburg] was burned down. They are going to rebuild it. Some of the boys have subscribed to help build a new one.

How hard it rains. We are confined to our tents. Such days is well adapted to make one lonesome, but fortunately, I am not of that turn of mind, but many a poor fellow will get home sick to day for he had no employment and is confined to his tent. His mind will, in spite of him, wander back to the North and his pleasant home and the many friends there. He will long to see them and when he thinks it is impossible at the present and the state of our once happy country, he will feel lonesome. But least you think me in that fix to day, I will say no more on that subject. I received a letter a day or two ago from home. They were all well. Well Mack, I have the association of some of our old collaborators and Fellows of Western Sun Lodge. I don't know whether you remember them or not. John Mooney, Dan Mead, Thom. Crull. They belong to the same company with me.

Well as I have wrote all of interest, I will close for the present hopeing to hear from you soon. I remain respectfully your Cousin,
George W. Montgomery.


## Western Sun Lodge 91

The issue of the burning of the Masonic Western Sun Lodge 91 in Wheelersburg was an important one, not only to its members but also to the entire community of Wheelersburg. Fellow lodge member, W. W. Merrill wrote to McLain Montgomery in response to his inquiries.

[Wheelers]Burg, Sunday June 28th 1863

Bro. Mc.

I received a letter from you last week for which you will accept the thanks of your humble servant and will be glad to hear from all the boys from about here never rec'd but one before and that from Ike [Pvt. Isaac Kennison, Company A]. A long time since I wrote to him and that is the last I heard from him. Give my best [re]spects to all the boys and tell them I would be happy to hear from all of them.

We have been having a good time with fire. First was the Hall & Pattens [Lemuel J. Patten's] grocery, J. Winkler's House [John L. Winkler], next Jack Enslows house and last if not least Murray's Store [Martin Murray, druggist], Zeke Coopers house and Sheds & Stable. They burned last Thursday night about 3 o'clock. Murray lost everything he had in the shop and about forty dollars in money he left in the drawer. It was most all U. S. currency change. Cooper lost his broom corn [millet] and a good many other things. The loss was heavy on both sides.

## The Portsmouth Times

### Destructive Fire at Wheelersburg.

WE regret to learn that our neighboring town of Wheelersburg was visited by a terrible fire on Thursday morning which destroyed some of the most valuable property in the place. The fire was discovered about two o'clock, A. M., in the roof of the Masonic Hall, which was soon enveloped in flames. The building, a large brick, and the finest in the place, was totally destroyed.— The goods of Mr. S. N. BRUNER, who kept a dry goods and grocery store in the lower story, were nearly all saved.— The flames communicated to the store of LEMUEL J. PATTON which, with a large portion of his goods, was consumed. The residence of JOHN L. WINKLER, adjoining, was also destroyed. The loss is estimated at $5,000 or $6,000.— A meeting of the lodge had been held on the previous evening, (Wednesday,) and the fire is supposed to have been communicated to the roof through a defective flue. The entire property of the Fraternity, including the furniture of the Hall, was lost. This catastrophe will be a severe blow to them as they have been struggling for some time to get out of debt and had almost succeeded.

*The* Portsmouth Times, *Saturday, April 4, 1863.*

During the Civil War, most druggists manufactured their own remedies from local plants and herbs. Another staple used to treat disease and wounds was whisky. The availability of this tonic made drugstores a favorite place for some locals.

The fire started in Murrays and he says the Republican party set it on fire and Zeke Powers, Finch [Cyrus M. Finch] and others of the party make a great hue & cry about it politically. I think if it was set on fire, it was done by someone that he has insulted by not letting them have whiskey. But who or what party that one belonged to is not known. I suppose they think that it will make their side more votes if they can get honest men to think the Republican party are a set of house burners, but I hope we have no one here so shallow minded as to believe a thing of the kind. I tell you what is a fact. There is a set of dry looking fellows here since the fire because they can't get anything to drink.

Old Singer is about played out in the grocery line. It is about all hardware, such as old stoves and other scrap iron. He done a pretty good business for a while but he has let his stock run down. I expect for want of funds and Batten won't sell anything strong. H. [Horace] F. Hall & Jas. Patingale are in the Dry goods trade together and I am clerking for them at present. [Owen] Bruner is fixing up his brick next to Halls for a storeroom. He has gained his land suit so I expect he will open out again in full blast soon if he is not broke. For certain there is a good many Butternuts here this season, or Valandinghamers [*sic*], whichever you may call them and I wouldn't wonder if we would have a warm time as they are talking all the time to get up an excitement between the parties.

The contract for building [a] New Hall was to have been let out yesterday but we only got two bids and they were too high for the money we have got subscribed so we will have to have more money or wait until labor and materials get lower than they are at present. The plan we have will make a nicer house & hall for us than the other was. Not quite so large, 50 ft. by 25 t., three stories high to enter at side at back corner so we won't have to pass through middle hall to get to lodge room. There will be a raise all round the room to set the chairs on. Master's Stand, three steps. S.W. [Senior Warden] two steps, J.W. [Junior Warden] one step higher. That sized room will be better for us than one as large as the one we had before. I think so at least. Don't you? I think we can get enough money to build if everyone does his best which we all ought to do. But if we can't get enough to build without going into debt again, we will have to take off one story or cut it down some other way. We must have a place to meet or else give up trying to keep up a lodge here. If you get any money send it over as fast as you get it so we will know what we can do. The Trustees may let the job, yet they think they can get one man down to twenty-eight hundred. If they can they will go right on with the work. I am Secretary & Treasurer of the Committee so you can express all money to me or any one of us here or send it the best

way you think of to get here safe and don't give up as long as you can get a dollar. We have sent circulars to most all the lodges in the state but have not had time to hear from them yet.
Write soon.
Fraternally
W.W. Merrill

The following letter from McLain's sister-in-law Abigail Hastings Montgomery, shared news of her siblings: Hulda, Anna, Eliza, Ursula, and Samantha, as well as news of other family members.

Sunday, July 12, 1863
Dear Brother McLain
We received yours last night and hasten to reply. Yours was a long time a coming, but was none the less welcome for we are always anxious to hear form you. We are all well as

*Abigail Hastings Montgomery*

usual though Del is not very stout this summer. Mr. Janes has been quite sick, but is better now. We have had some very warm weather here already and it is very dry so that some of the wheat is entirely killed with the drought. The war news seems very favorable lately and I hope to goodness it may continue to be favorable until we have an end, if there is to be an end at all. But I have always been impatient about it from the beginning. Samantha and Ursula have been down here to spend the fourth. They are both big girls. They work out[side]. Huldah is at Eliza's and Ann is with us. McNitts folks are all or was a week ago. My maw is still improving in her lazyness so they tell me you pretend today there may be an outcome to her yet. Well that may be but still she will never make a neat or industrious woman while she lives. No sir, tain't in the book and you need not preach it to me. Father is still living with Elijah at Amboy. I don't know much about how they are a getting along. You wished me to find out why Adeline don't write to you. The last time I say [to her] she told me she had answered your last letter & sent you her mother's picture and as for John he is always slow and has been laid up with a sore hand. Newton, I have not seen for some time and so I have no excuse for him, and so if I see him I will attend to giving him that spanking you spoke of.

Now brother, tell your wife not to be putting such nonsense into your head as to make you think your child is pretty for that was the way you wrote it. There is no pretty children but mine and she does look like her father for she is bald headed, blackeyed, long-legged and long chined. There, that is a complete description. Now don't go to copying this and sending it home to ask your wife if yours ain't like her, for I know she ain't for in the first place she ain't bald, for you sent some of her hair and there too she don't look like you for you are bald, did you know it? Well I do if you don't, but don't make up your mind that I think you any the better of being bald headed just because Del is inclined a little that way. Well, I am almost to the end of this sheet and will have to close. Give my love to your wife and baby if she ain't pretty. And to all the soldiers in the camp, Generals Grant and Rosecrans, in particular and accept of a sisters love for yourself. No more from me but Del will write though.
Yours Sister
Abigail A. Montgomerie

## John Hunt Morgan's Raid Through Southern Ohio

On July 30, Sergeant Montgomery received a letter from Mary Ann in which she talked about the notorious foray of Confederate Morgan and his raiders through southern Ohio. From June 11 until his capture on July 26, 1863, Confederate brigadier general John Hunt Morgan lead a cavalry raid through southern Indiana and Ohio. The raid which occurred roughly at the same time as the Vicksburg and Gettysburg campaigns, aroused Union fears and resulted in the deployment of thousands of Union troops into southern Ohio in pursuit to prevent Morgan from fording the Ohio River at Buffington Island. On July 26, Morgan and his remaining men (about four hundred) were defeated near New Lisbon, Ohio. Morgan and his officers were imprisoned in the Ohio Penitentiary in Columbus, Ohio, while most of his enlisted men were sent to Camp Douglas, Chicago, Illinois. On November 4, Morgan and six of his officers began digging a tunnel. Finally, on November 26 their work of tunneling into the prison yard was complete. The following night, under cover of darkness and a steady rain they entered the yard and climbed out over the prison wall. Morgan and all but two of his officers successfully escaped back to Tennessee.

Camp near Cowan, Tenn. July 31, 1863

Dear Wife. Your letter came safe to hand yesterday and I was glad indeed to hear from you after so long a time. It took a load of anxious thoughts from my mind and I feel content now that I know that you and Ella is well. When I heard that Morgan was in Ohio I was very uneasy for fear he would prey on our neighbors (?) How I longed to be near you but thank God his career is ended at least for a while and I hope forever. I am glad to hear that some of our copperhead neighbors has to shoulder the musket and to trust John Morgan's raid in Ohio will give some of the peace men a little idea of what we are undergoing to protect them. I suppose Frank will be a little more careful in future how he talks before [he] knows who he is talking to.

It reminds me of a little incident that is said to have taken place in Hamilton County. A fine old butternut gentleman was called upon by Morgan who was hospitably fed [and] received the old man's blessing. The old man was possessed of eight fine horses. Now John was covetous and proposed taking them. The old man protested against if and finally prevailed on John to divide and take but four. After it was agreed to the old man asked John how he could manage to keep the men that was still behind from taking them, John told him to holler for Vallandingham and Davis. John then left, leaving the old man to holler for the protection of his remaining four horses. In a short time, General [Edward Henry] Hobson passed that way in pursuit of Morgan and the old man, thinking they was John's men, cheered lustily for Jeff and Vallandingham, whereupon Hobson insisted on taking the remaining four horses so leaving the old man cursing both Union men and rebels. But my paper is most full so I will change the subject.

We are now in a nice clean camp and have enough to eat. We have black berries every day. James and I are both in good health. I got

*Albina Montgomery Janes*

a letter from Ill's yesterday. They are all well. Sister Albina sent me her picture. I will send it to you. Now Dear Mary, my love to mother and the rest of the family and my blessing on you and Ella and my prayers for your safety. Good by. Direct Co. A 33rd OV.I, 1st Brig. 1st Div. 14th A.C.
Cowan, Tenn.

## Rosecrans Finally on the Move

By late summer, General Rosecrans had finally decided it was time to move out, and the Army of the Cumberland left Murfreesboro on the Manchester pike towards Hoover's Gap. Over the next few days they successfully forced the rebels to relinquish control of Hoover's and Liberty Gap and had forced General Bragg to continue to retreat southward. During this time the regiment had faced heavy fire from Confederate batteries. One of those injured was Cpl. Samuel Roxby, Company A. who wrote to alert Sergeant Montgomery to his condition.

Aug. 1st 1863 Nashville, Tenn
Sir: I wrote you a letter to you last week. I do not believe it left here for it had no stamp on it. I did not know that a letter could not be sent to the front without a stamp on it until after it was in the office. I received your letter of the 9th of June the day I left the

field hospital some eight days ago. I am at present in Hospital 14, Ward No. 1. I am getting some better. My leg feels weak yet it is getting better. My eye sight has returned as good as ever I have no news to send you but what you have heard before this. Except that I am out of money and tobacco so I sent you to ask Mr [Phineas] Hawkins for that money he owes me. Tell him I am out of money and have not been paid. I should like to have it. If there are any letters there for me please send them. When you write, let me know if the Capt has had an answer to that letter. You know what I mean. This is my last sheet of paper and a last stamp so you know how I want money. Write me a long letter as soon as you get his. Ask Byron Orm if he knows where Funk [James J. Funk, Private Co. A, discharged August 8, 1863, on Surgeon's Certificate of disability] is. I hear he has been discharged and gone home. Give my respects to all.

Yours respectfully

Samuel Roxby

# CHAPTER 9

# Reports From Alabama and Ohio

## Anderson Station

As Sergeant Montgomery and the men of the Thirty-third began to move south again, Mary's concern for his safety intensified. She felt relief upon reading her husband's letter from Anderson Station, Tennessee, for he clearly missed her, but was dismayed whenever he expressed doubts as to his continued ability to survive whatever mortal threats he might face on the field of battle.

Anderson Station, Tenn. Aug. 9, 1863

Dear Wife.

I shall wait no longer for an answer to my last but write and let you know that I am still in good health. My last letter was written at Cowan, since then we have moved about seventeen miles farther across the mountains. Our camp is now in Alabama. We are just over the line. Anderson Station is less than half a mile distant in Tenn.

We are only ten miles distant from Stevenson so you see we are getting nearly back to last summer's quarters. We are very pleasantly situated here in a grove of heavy beech timber on the banks of Crow Creek and almost surrounded by the Cumberland Mountains. We are living tolerable well at present. They give us green corn every day and we help ourselves to peaches and such other articles as comes in our way. How long we will stay here is hard to tell. We may leave tomorrow and we may stay here a month or longer.

While I was at Cowan Station I sent 40 dollars home in your name. It was left in care of Ben Miles in Portsmouth. I should have sent more, but I was unfortunate when crossing Elk River where we had to wade breast deep. I lost my pocket book with $18. Now dear Mary, do not reproach me for carelessness for I could not help it. I feel the loss keenly on yours and Ella's account well knowing that I will need every cent I can get for your comfort, and your happiness, dear Mary shall be my chief goal through life. You and my darling child fill my thought by day and when night comes I visit you in my dreams and am happy but morning comes and brings the sad reality back to me that I am far, far away. But Mary if it is the Lord's will that I should live and be happy as to return to you, nothing but the dire necessity can ever convince me to leave you again. But providence has smiled on me thus far. I have passed through many dangers unscathed and I trust that God's mercy will shield me and keep me in future for yours and [for] Ella's sake, not mine.

Pray for me Mary that I may be able to put my trust more fully in Him who has power over all things on earth. And you can tell mother that James is well. He has gone out to dig some potatoes and get some peaches to cook for dinner. He commenced to write a letter to mother the day that we left Cowan, but did not get to finish it. I will try and get him at it again this afternoon.

When you write again, you must tell me all about Jesse's soldiering and also the soldier's wife. When you write direct to Anderson station, Tenn. Give my love to mother and kiss Ella for me and let me hear from you often. Good by, God bless you.
Yours true and faithful
Mc to Mary


## Ohio Militia and Morgan's Raid

The inquiry regarding the experiences of Mary's sister Cynthia and her thirty-six-year-old "soldier" husband, Jesse Rowley, carried a bit of sarcasm. Mary had written to McLain about Scioto County men in the Ohio Militia and of the importance her sister placed on her husband Jesse's new duty.

On August 11, Masonic brother, W. W. Merrill wrote to McLain to describe his own experiences as part of the First Scioto Militia unit that had been called to duty in response to Morgan's raid. Clearly Merrill had a sense of humor as he joked about his own expectations for personal glory.

The Ohio Militia had undergone a much-needed reorganization in January of 1863. By law, all able-bodied men between the ages of eighteen and forty-five were required to enroll; however, it was understood that they would only be called in the event of an attack on their homes and communities. The threat presented by Morgan's incursion into southern Ohio precipitated such a call for the militia. On July 14, Col. Peter Kinney of the Fifty-sixth Regiment Ohio Volunteer Infantry was ordered by Governor David Tod to assume command of the more than 350 men of the volunteer militia at Portsmouth. One day later Kinney received authority from Maj. Gen. Ambrose E. Burnside to declare martial law in Portsmouth under Burnside's name if deemed necessary. Details of Kinney's actions were provided in his official report of the event.

Kinney had immediately sent couriers to every neighborhood within twenty miles requesting that citizens assist in the blockading of roads by felling trees in order to delay Morgan's advance. By July 16 Morgan had reached the small town of Jasper along the Scioto River in neighboring Pike County and the level of panic increased. Kinney had distributed to the militiamen the limited arms available to him. These included about three hundred muskets, which Kinney described as inferior and one brass 6-pounder that had been condemned as unfit for service. There was much speculation regarding the route Morgan would follow, but as a precaution, Kinney declared martial law in Portsmouth and sent Lt. Col. Sampson Varner of the Fifty-sixth Ohio with a detachment of three hundred men toward Jasper.

By July 17, word reached Kinney that Morgan had already crossed the Scioto River and had moved east in the direction of Jackson, and Lt. Col. Sampson Varner and his men were ordered back to Portsmouth. That same day one thousand muskets arrived from Columbus and the volunteers received the new arms. By this time, there were nearly five thousand men in camp. According to Kinney, since he did not have enough arms for all of them, he discharged those who were unarmed. His rationale was that they would be of more service by getting in their crops than if they were to remain lying idle in camp at the state's expense.

Late in the evening of Sunday, July 19, Kinney received word that a portion of Morgan's command was near Jackson. Kinney then ordered Lt. Col. Louis Sontag to take a detachment of five hundred men from the First Scioto Militia by train to Jackson where he was to send out small scouting parties of no more than thirty-five men to search the hills around the approach to Jackson for signs of the raiders. For some unknown reason, Sontag disobeyed orders and divided his command in half and left half of those men at Keystone Station under Maj. Jackson Slane with orders to march to Ewington in Gallia County. Sontag moved on toward Jackson and from there marched to Ewington Monday night. The men of the newly organized militia were untrained and undisciplined. They were unaccustomed to such duty and many lagged behind complaining of sore feet and no rations.

Early the following morning, a part of Morgan's command entered Ewington. Sontag had failed to place pickets around his perimeter, was taken by surprise, and surrendered his command without giving any resistance. If that weren't bad enough, Sontag then proceeded to inform Morgan of the location of Major Slane's men, who were also captured without resistance. Later reports revealed that only a small portion of Morgan's men were armed and those that were had but limited ammunition. Along with the militiamen, Morgan captured 395 French rifled muskets and fifteen thousand rounds of ammunition. Needless to say, charges were filed against both Sontag and Slane.

Although the Confederate raiders had, without any difficulty at all, captured the militiamen, Morgan's plans called for lightning movement of his men and the burden of captured enemy posed a problem. The solution was to parole the recent captives and send them home.

On Wednesday, July 22, 1863, Kinney, by order of Governor Tod, disbanded the Portsmouth camp and sent the men back to their homes. Although the raid had generated a great deal of anxiety and excitement, Scioto County emerged unscathed by Morgan's advance, while neighboring counties of Adams and Pike lay directly in the raiders' path.

Lodge brother W. W. Merrill welcomed the opportunity to share news of his own militia experience during the raid. His letter indicates that their designation had been elevated to Company A, First Ohio Militia and that the current officers were all residents of Wheelersburg.

Wheelersburg, O. Aug. 11, 1863

Bro. Mc.

I rec'd your communication with check for $105 enclosed for Western Sun Ledge No. 91, F. & A.M. and have neglected to write sooner. Some days I am pretty busy in the store and haven't time to write and some days too lazy and then the Morgan Raid has been the talk & thoughts for a while past. I was in camp a week at the time he was around and if our company hadn't been quite so late we would have been one of the no. that were surrendered to Morgan under Col. Sontag. We belonged to his Regt. But didn't get out in time to take our place and got into the other Regt. & stopped at Portland. That is all that saved us.

We were Co. D., 1st Ohio Militia but we have since raised a notch to Co. A. Capt. J. S. Whitney Act. Colonel until our reg't is organized & field officers are elected, which will be the last of this month or first of next. I don't know who our field officers will be. Expect I shall be Briger Dier Gineral or some higher officer. Maybe president instead of Lincoln or Jeff Davis. Our Company officers are Capt. J. S. Whitney, 1st Lieut. Wm. Webb, 2nd Lieut Levi Wheeler, Orderly S. M. W. Merrill and you better believe it is a heavy company. You better send your Co. up and take lessons from us in the various maneuvering of Co. & Regimental Drill.

## Ohio's Gubernatorial Election

Merrill was curious about the attitudes of the men of the Thirty-third regarding the upcoming gubernatorial contest between Republican nominee John Brough and Democrat nominee Clement Laird Vallandigham. Vallandigham had won a seat in the U.S. House of Representatives in 1858 and became notorious as a vocal opponent of the war. In April of 1863, in a speech in Columbus, Ohio, he made derogatory remarks about President Lincoln and the war effort. This was an intentional violation of General Order No. 38 issued by Maj. Gen. Ambrose E. Burnside, Department of the Ohio, which outlawed any expression of support for the enemy. As a result of his speech, he was arrested at his home in Dayton, Ohio, on May 5 and tried by a military court. The court found him guilty and he was sentenced to two years in a military prison; however, President Lincoln commuted his sentence and banished him to the Confederacy. Democrats were so angered by the treatment Vallandigham had received that they nominated him as their candidate for governor. In the election, Brough defeated Vallandigham by a margin of more than one hundred thousand votes.

> How is Brough & Val going to make it with you folks? I think we will come out all right. There are some strong Butternuts around here, but it will soon be time for cracking about October they will all be played out. I heard the butternuts had a basket meeting out at Harrisonvlle, Saturday to nominate County officers and made a ticket as follows: for Rep. S. Varner; Treas—Hitchcook; Clerk, B. F. Cunningham; Probate judge, Frank Batterson; Prosecuting Attorney, G. P. Newman; Commissioner, Violet. Our ticket is as follows; Rep, Eli Glover; Treas, Ward; Clerk, Drouliard; Probate Judge, F. C. Searl; Pros. Attor, Harper; Commissioner, Jackson. I think the last ticket will be elected by a larger majority than it or any other party has had for a long time. As far as I can hear there is but few Valandinghamers in the service. They have seen enough to convince them of the error of their ways and a good many of the leaders at home will die a natural death. Lots of them will never be elected for any office after this war is over. Some I have voted for heretofore. I shall never give them a vote again unless I change my mind more than I think I shall.

We have not let the contract to build our Hall yet. It was to have been let some time ago, but the bids were too high for our money so we will have to cut the Hall down some or wait till Material gets lower. There is a man in Portsmouth thinks he can build us a House that will suit us for 27 or 28 hundred dollars and promised to come up and see about it. If he does, he will commence it this fall and finish next spring. It is about mail time.

Give my respects to all the boys and write soon.

Fraternally Yours

W. W. Merrill to McLean Montgomery

———————

Camp near Anderson Station, Tenn.
August 17, 1863

Dear wife. Three or four days since I rec'd a letter from you bearing the welcome news that all was well, but as I had just written a day or two before, I have put off answering it til now, and now I fear my letter will be dull and uninteresting for the want of news, but I know the simple words [that] I am well will give you pleasure enough to pay me for writing.

We are still at Anderson Station, but I think we will make a forward movement before long, perhaps as far as Bridgeport or Battle Creek. I dread the move. It is so warm but the march is not likely to be very long and we may get a more desirable place for our encampment. We have sent men back to Ohio to get conscripts to fill up our regiment, so I think our duty will be much lighter this fall and winter than it has been. I have not heard from George since the latter part of June. I answered his letter immediately but he has never written since. If you have heard [from] him, let me know where he is and I will write to him again, and also give me his regimental address as I have lost it and forgotten it. I rec'd a letter from Adaline Janes a few days since. All was well, except sister Albina. She had been quite sick but was much better.

The brief statement below is yet another reference to the unexpected marriage of his young niece Loraine to the widower Oliver H. Hastings in Illinois. Fifteen-year-old Loraine found herself faced with the responsibilities of caring for four of Oliver's nine children who were still living at home. These included thirteen-year-old twins,

Ursula and Hulda, ten-year-old Anna and seven-year-old Robert.

> From all I can learn, my new nephew and his wife are not likely to make very great headway in this life. It is quite evident that her stepchildren do not like her and her experience as a housekeeper is spoken very lightly of. But if they are satisfied, I had ought to be.

Sergeant Montgomery was optimistic about the possibility of a speedy end to the war and seemed to feel for the first time since the outbreak of war, that things were going "decidedly" in favor of the Union army. Perhaps his mood was improved by the abundance of food so readily available to them on their foraging expeditions.

> Yesterday I was out on a pass. I went out for the purpose of getting some of the groceries of the season for a change in living. I brought in potatoes, apples and peaches. James and I are in the same mess now. While he was paring some of the apples for cooking, he said he would like a few quarts of milk from home so he could have some dumplings, but if nothing happens, this time next year we can eat dumplings at home and I think much sooner. The clouds of war appear to be breaking away and I hope the sunshine of peace will soon lighten our way home and warm the hearts of those that have waited for us so patiently at home. I have good reason for to hope for never since the rebellion broke out has everything appeared to be so decidedly in our favor as it is at this time. But I have written a much longer letter than I designed so I will close by requesting you to give my love to Mother and all the rest at home.

Although Sergeant Montgomery's older brother, John S. Montgomery, had moved from Wheelersburg to Illinois in the 1840s, he apparently still cherished fond memories of his childhood days on Dogwood Ridge.

> Tell father that John Montgomery sends his best wishes to him and says he would like once more to visit Dogwood Ridge and see all of the folks. Now Dear Wife, kiss my little girl for me and write to your absent husband very often. May the blessings of an ever indulgent God be with you and shield you from all harm is the prayer of your devoted husband.
> Mc Montgomery to Mary
> Camp of the 33rd OVI near Anderson station Tenn.

During his lengthy stay at Murfreesboro, Tennessee, in the early months of 1863, Gen. William Starke Rosecrans had devoted much time and numerous communications with General Halleck in his attempts to obtain more horses for his command. Rosecrans was convinced that mounted troops were essential for his efforts to combat opposition from Confederate cavalry units in Tennessee. He had even gone so far as to dispatch Maj. Gen. Lovell H. Rousseau to Washington, D.C., in a lobbying effort to gain support for his proposal. His inability to adequately care for those horses that were sent to him resulted in increased dissatisfaction from his superiors and ultimately with their decision to withhold the shipment of more animals.

August 27th, 1863
Dear Wife. I have waited long and patiently for a letter from home but it appears I am still to wait. Sometimes I fear you are sick and then I think perhaps you don't get my letters, for I am sure, my Dear Mary has not forgot me. I wrote to you just before I rec'd your last letter and then I answered yours but have got no reply. I will have to give you a short letter this time for the want of anything interesting to write. We are still in our old camp with fair prospects of staying here for some time.

There is some talk of our Division being mounted, but it is hard to tell what will be done with us. Yet we are having [a] very easy time at present. Our duty is light and we have plenty to eat. We have green beans and sweet potatoes, green corn, peaches and pumpkins. James is now preparing to cook a pumpkin for our dinner. We have plenty of sugar and coffee and bread and meat. If I could only hear from home a bit oftener, I would be as well contented here as I could any place away from you.

But my three years is fast passing away and if I meet with no accident this time next year, I will be with you and I hope much sooner. And if I ever get home again, I will never leave it unless compelled to. I have not heard from Ill's since I wrote to you. I guess they have forgot me. And I have heard nothing from George. Now Mary, for fear you have not received my last letter, I will tell you how to direct. Co. A, 33rd, 1st Brig, 1st Div., 14th A.C., Anderson Station, Tenn. This leaves me well but very anxious about you and Ella. James is well and sends his love. Walter McNeal [1st Lieut. Company A] sends his respects. If you can,

Mary, send me your likeness. I had the misfortune to lose the one I had. Give my love to Mother and write to me soon.
From your devoted husband. Mc Mont to Mary

## Trouble on the Home Front

Any news from the front was eagerly awaited including letters from her brother, George of the Thirty-ninth Ohio. In the following letter George notified Mary of the death of Pvt. James Freeland of Company C, Thirty-ninth Ohio Infantry who, according to his service record, died from disease on July 26, 1863, at Memphis, Tennessee.

> August 30, 1863
> Mary, your letter bearing date of 23 of August is before me. I hasten to answer it. Was glad to hear from you and the rest of the folks and to hear that you and the rest was well for I am not well now have not been for some time. Tell Mother that James Fr[e]eland is dead. The loss of his death was from a wound he got in the fight at Corinth. He never was well. Since that there is a great deal of sickness here. At present the nights here are so cold it makes one [think] of home and the old fire place instead of the woods and the open tents. I will stop. You may think me homesick. Not so.

George expressed some concern that his sisters Mary Ann and Cynthia were having some personal problems with his wife, Mary. It is unclear from the following portion of the letter exactly who was squabbling with whom, but the situation was of concern to George. At the time, his wife Mary Catharine was residing within the household of his sister Mary Ann.

> Mary, you said if I would write you would tell me something that I think is not so. Tell me the news, all, for I want to hear what the news is. Tell me all when you write.

> Mary I was sorry to hear what I did from home that you and Mary and Cintha could not get along any better than you do. Mary you wanted to know who wrote it to me. It was not wrote at all, for it was told me by one that was home on furlough. Mary, I will say no more about this at present.

Write all the news. I have had no letter from Mack nor James for some time. I don't know what the matter is. We was paid the other day and I will [send] the certificate in this letter. Give it to Mother for me. She can get it by going to the County Treasurer. Write soon as you can. I send $55 dollars.

G.W. M.

Mary A. Montgomery

(George Montgomery to sister, Mary)

———————

Anderson Station

August 30th 1863

Dear wife, Yesterday I rec'd your letter dated the 23rd and I was indeed rejoiced to learn that you and my pet was well and the picture that I found enclosed paid me for waiting so long for a letter. I had just written a letter to you complaining a little about your not writing. I did not then know that the welcome messenger was so near at hand and you cannot tell the good it has done me. For the last week or two I could be seen setting away by myself, so cross and non sociable that I was no company for anyone and each morning when the mail was handed around, I would stand and listen till the last name was called and failing to get the long looked for letter, I would turn away to hide my disappointment. One night while I slept I dreamed the mail came in and I thought there was a letter for me. I thought I opened it and tried to read it but the lines would fade away before my eyes and at last I thought I held a blank sheet in my hand. The next morning I had no patience to wait for the mail and thought the hours of double length until mail came. When the letters was called off, I heard my name among the rest. I was so eager to get my letter that some of the boys noticed it and said the old Sergeant has come to life. He had got a letter. But, when I found the Nashville Postmark on it instead of the Wheelersburg stamp, I was almost as much disappointed as though I had rec'd the blank sheet of my dream. But, thanks to you, Dear Mary, your kind and affectionate letter has dispelled my gloomy thoughts and I am as happy as I ever expect to be while absent from you. I have to look at my Ella's picture a dozen times a day. You must give her a dozen kisses for me, but save a few for me when I come. I have nothing new to write this time, but I shall expect another letter from you before long.

It is strange about George requesting his wife to have nothing to do with you. Perhaps she has been writing something to him. Maybe that is the reason that she has not answered my letter. Good bye Dearest Mary. Give my love to mother and tell her I will try and prevail on James to write today or tomorrow. We are both well. Yours affectionately
Mc to Mary

As the Thirty-third prepared to move toward Chattanooga, Sergeant Montgomery reflected on the prospect of another encounter with the Confederate forces under Braxton Bragg and expressed surprise over the condition of the terrain over which they were passing. He noted that the devastation of the land was far greater than he could ever have imagined.

By the roadside above Stevenson, Alabama
Sep. 2nd, 1863
Dear Wife, Yesterday we broke up our camp and turned our faces southward. The grand Army of the Cumberland is on the move again. I believe our destination is Chattanooga. Our troops have been crossing the Tennessee River since last Friday. It has been thought that Chattanooga would be taken without much of a fight. How it will be, I can't tell, but from all appearances we will soon find out. But I do not fear for the result. We have whipped Bragg three times and we feel like we could do it again. We are now on ground that we are well acquainted with. We are now within a few miles of Fort McCook where we was shelled out of last year, but how changed the country since we left.

I thought we left the country in a deplorable condition. I had no idea that it could be much worse, but the condition now surpasses anything I ever saw. There is not a farm that has escaped and hardly a family is left. What few there is has to depend chiefly on our troops for support. We yesterday passed the village of Boliver. There is not a single family left in the place and the houses is nothing but a mass of ruins. But enough of this, my seat is rather uncomfortable so I will have to be brief.

We have just turned aside here to wait for some repairs on the bridges across the river. We will leave here tomorrow morning and perhaps sooner. Our march this far has been very fatiguing on account of the dust which is very deep and light, but thank God I am in good health and we have plenty to eat. Last night I succeeded in getting a good mess of sweet potatoes. We found a patch that had so far escaped, but the soldiers that comes along there hereafter will not fare so well. There was about half an acre in the patch and it was dug all over. Well, Dear Mary, you see I am near the end of my paper so you will excuse me for not writing more. Give my love to mother. Tell her James is well. Kiss my Ella for me and believe me ever faithful.

Mc Montgomery to Mary

Direct as I last told you until I tell you different. I will write again as soon as we get in camp, but you need not wait. You can write anytime and the letter will come.

Your devoted Husband

Mc Montgomery to Mary Montgomery

**CHAPTER 10**

# Battle of Chickamauga, Georgia

## The Lull Before the Storm

Camp in Lachramose [McLemore's] Cove, Georgia
Sept 16th 1863
Dear wife. Day before yesterday I received a letter from you bearing date Sept. 3rd. I was happy indeed to hear that you and Ella was well. I got your letter with her picture and it did pay me for waiting. I have to take a look at it every day. Now, if I had her mother's picture to carry with it I would be satisfied. You want to know how I want your picture? In [a] case or without. I would rather have it like Ella's then I can carry it better with less danger of losing it.

I have written once since I have left Anderson and would have written again but I have not had an opportunity. We have been on the move all most every day since we left. We have not marched very hard but our road has been a very rough one over mountains and through the dust. It has been very dry and warm. We are not in camp yet. We have just turned aside in the woods. We have not put up our tents nor will not unless it rains for we are under orders to be ready to move at a moments notice. We found a corps of rebels here in the cove. We fought them on the 10th. That was day before yesterday. We did not have a general engagement and the loss of life on either side was not heavy. We expected to fight them on the 13th but they left us in the night and it is not likely we will overtake them for some time.

Lachramose [McLemore's] Cove where we are in camp is between Lookout Mountain and Pidgeon Mountain. It is a rich valley and would be a desirable place to live in times of peace. At the present it looks deserted and lonely. Yesterday I saw two women and one young man that had been three or four days in the mountains hiding from the rebels. They had been without food for two days. The man was a paroled prisoner from Vicksburg. He thinks the rebellion is about played out. I think so too. Our men are gaining victories every day and the rebels appear to be growing discouraged. I hope another half year will put an end to our trials. That old flag you spoke of Mary is the pride of the 33rd although the battle rents in it are numerous, it has never been disgraced and next to my dear ones at home, I love the old flag the best. Now Mary I will bid you good bye. Write often and direct as before until I tell you different. This leaves me (?) one kiss for Ella and my blessing on you both.
Yours ever true
Mc Montgomery to Mary

To Mother
Dear mother, you wanted me to see James about writing. I did get him to write just before we left Anderson. I expect you have got his letter long before this. I would write for him and write oftener but I . . .

A few days after writing this last letter, the Thirty-third Ohio again confronted Confederate forces in two of the bloodiest days of the war. On September 19 and 20, as part of the Army of the Cumberland's Fourteenth Corps under Maj. Gen. George H. Thomas, they would fight at the "River of Death" in the battle of Chickamauga, Georgia.

## Battle of Chickamauga, Georgia

Although the first day of battle was hard fought by both armies, the second day proved to be disastrous for the Union forces. At about eleven o'clock in the morning of September 20, Major General William Starke Rosecrans, still in command of the Army of the Cumberland, received faulty intelligence that led him to believe that his troops were not aligned according to his orders. He was informed that there was a gap in his battle line and consequently moved forces to fill that gap. In reality, what he did was to create a gap where none had existed before. Confederate general Longstreet plunged into that gap and effectively routed nearly half of the Union forces. Rosecrans, himself, was among those who retreated in ragged disarray back toward Chattanooga. During the afternoon of September 20, Major General George H. Thomas steadfastly held the area around Snodgrass Hill with the center of the Fourteenth Army Corps, and earned for himself, the reputation as "the Rock of Chickamauga."

Included in that number of Thomas's men was the Thirty-third Ohio regiment under the command of Col. Oscar F. Moore. They were a part of the First division under Brig. Gen. Absalom Baird, First Brigade under Brig. Gen. Benjamin F. Scribner. The brigade consisted of five regiments: Thirty-eighth Indiana, Second Ohio, Thirty-third Ohio, Ninety-fourth Ohio, and Tenth Wisconsin.

The battle raged until dusk and although the order was given for the Union troops to fall back, they were unable to hear or understand the orders due to the noise and confusion of battle. Consequently, they continued to stubbornly hold their ground until, as Colonel Moore wrote in his official report: "they were completely surrounded and either killed, wounded, or captured."

Union casualties in that battle totaled 16, 200. Confederate forces reported 18,454 casualties. The Fourteenth Army Corps reported a loss of 6,114 men with 181 of those being from Baird's First Division. The Thirty-third Ohio suffered 15 killed, 93 wounded and 88 captured. Of those captured, 52 percent died in Confederate prisons.

Sergeant Montgomery was wounded slightly in the arm on the second day of fighting, but remained with the regiment. James Montgomery came through the fight unscathed. In the following letter, Sergeant Montgomery wrote to Mary to provide details of the battle. He felt certain that she would already have heard news of the battle and knew that she would be frightened and worried.

Chattanooga, Tenn
Sept 25th 1863

Dear Wife. I have but a few moments to devote to writing but as I expect you are anxious about me and James I will write a few lines. We both escaped unharmed through the dreadful conflict of the 19th & 20th. I have no time for particulars. Our loss was heavy. More than half of our company is killed, wounded or missing. Wm Fullerton was killed; Captain Singer [John P., Co. A] was wounded and is a prisoner. The loss of our reg't is 162. The rebels is threatening us again, but it is hardly probable they will fight us here behind our fortifications. At all events we are ready for them if they choose to make the attack. I would have written to you sooner if it had been possible, but it has not. I rec'd yours of the 10th and I am hopefully waiting for an answer to one that I wrote on the 15th. If we get settled soon, I will give you the particulars of the battle which was one of the bloodiest that it has been my lot to participate in. I got a slight hurt on the left arm, but it was of no consequence. I was fit for duty three hours after I rec'd it, but I will have to leave off for the present. This has been hastily written but perhaps you can read enough of it to understand that I am well. I am sorry I can't say as much for James. He has the ague every day. He is now sleeping off the fever from his chill today. Give my love to mother, kiss Ella for me and write soon. Direct to Chattanooga, Tenn. Good bye. God bless you from your devoted husband.
Mc Montgomery to Mary Montgomery

Mary Ann was relieved to receive word from her husband for she had, indeed, been worried. She could not be certain if he were telling her the truth about the severity of his wound, but she was comforted nonetheless. When she received another letter a little over a week later, she felt a little calmer. She was surprised at the matter-of-fact tone with which her husband detailed the events of the battle. The more of the letter she read, the more fearful she became.

Headquarters,
Co. A, 33rd Regiment Ohio Vol. Infantry,
Camp Near Chattanooga, Sept 30th 1863

Dear Wife. I wrote a few lines to you in haste a few days since expecting to have written again ere this but it has been a busy time with me. I could not write sooner. I promised to give you some of the particulars of our last bloody battle, but my time is limited so the details in this will in consequence be brief.

On the morning of the 19th we were camped in Chickamauga Valley 18 miles south of Chattanooga. We could hear skirmishing to the north of us and the occasional roar of artillery all day. In the evening we marched in that direction but owing to the darkness we traveled slow and at day light we had only marched about 10 miles. We got our breakfast about 8 o'clock. In the meantime, Reynold's [Maj. Gen. Joseph J. Reynolds] Division moved to the front to surround a brigade of rebels that was reported to be cut off. But the brigade turned out to be the whole of the rebel army of this department strengthened by 2 corps from Virginia. In about half an hour, Reynolds brought on the engagement and drove them. Our division was then led forward in the centre to protect Reynolds left flank and we did not get in position a moment too soon. We soon saw the rebels advancing in double column.

We was ordered to retain our fire until they come up close, which we did, [with] our first fire being delivered at a distance less than 75 yds. We was then exposed to the most deadly fire that I ever witnessed. For awhile our little brigade disputed every foot of ground, but being unsupported, we were forced to give way. Our company that morning lost in killed, wounded and missing, fifteen. Among the killed was Wm. Fullerton. Among the wounded, Cyrus Y. Gibbons [name listed as Stilson Gibbons on Adjutant General's report]. Some three or four hours was then occupied in gathering up our men. We then went to the front again. The fight had been kept up with the advantages on our side, we being in support of Davis's [Brig. Gen. Jefferson C. Davis] Division.

Just at dark we was attacked again and by such numbers that we was again forced back. During the fight in the dark I got a slight lick with a rifle ball, but fortunately the injury was so slight that the next morning found me ready to resume the fight. It commenced about 9 o'clock and raged during the remainder of the day.

Although I have told of the horrors of Stone River and Perryville, I found that I had yet to learn with what desperation men was capable of fighting with. The dead and wounded lay in piles over the field. Our men bravely held their ground against overwhelming numbers until our ammunition was exhausted and then fell back on Chattanooga followed up close by the enemy. But we have stopped here and we intend to stay here.

This place has cost the blood of too many brave men to give it up so soon. Every day makes us stronger and we feel strong enough to whip the whole southern confederacy if they will only fight us here. But you see my paper is full. I must quit. I commenced this yesterday. Today it is raining like fury. Give my love to Mother. Kiss my darling and write often. James and I are both well.
Your husband
Mc Montgomery to Mary Montgomery

As Mary finished the letter she was overcome with apprehension. How many more such battles could he survive? Would she ever see him again? Suddenly she found herself sobbing uncontrollably and little Ella, frightened by her mother's behavior began to cry as well. It would be another, long sorrowful night.

**CHAPTER 11**

# Under Siege at Chattanooga, Tennessee

## *Surrounded by Rebel Artillery*

General Rosecrans's blunder at Chickamauga, coupled with his hesitancy to advance for nearly six months after his success at Stones River, resulted in his removal from command of the Army of the Cumberland and Maj. Gen. George H. Thomas replaced him. Although the Union army had been soundly defeated at Chickamauga, they had retreated to Chattanooga and continued to hold that important supply hub of the Confederacy. Unfortunately, however, the Confederate forces of Braxton Bragg held strategic positions on Lookout Mountain and on Missionary Ridge and fortified them with artillery. They were thus in a superior tactical position to control any transportation of men or supplies into the city. Conditions in the beleaguered city worsened over the next month.

Sergeant Montgomery dutifully wrote to Mary and did not mention the dire circumstances they were facing at the time. He did confess to her that the brutality of war had made a lasting impression upon him.

Chattanooga, Tennessee, Oct. 5th A.D. 1863

Dear Wife. This is the third letter since I received one from you but do not think I am complaining for I do not intend to complain for the mails is very irregular and I am not sure that you are getting any word from me. That is the reason I do not wait for an answer from you, but if you rec'd my first letter after the battle I trust there is a letter some place on the road for me. Since I wrote last I have [been] quite unwell, but I am much better. James is hearty again and I think if we are allowed to rest here for a while we will fatten up enough to stand the coming winter tolerable well. Our last winter, I trust.

One year ago today, Mary I experienced my first hard battle. How different were the emotions that filled my breast at that time to those since then under similar circumstances. Then a bleeding soldier awakened the deepest sympathy and the gory corpses made me shudder and the sound of fire arms would stir up anxious thoughts. But Stone River and Chickamauga have either exhausted my stock of sympathy or deadened my feelings for humanity and which I can't tell. But I expect you would rather hear something of what is going on here than be bothered with my experience through the last bloody fight. But it is easy told. The sight [of] a dead soldier troubles me no more than the sight of a dead horse or any other animal, and as for the sound of fire arms, I can sleep as soundly with cannon thundering in my ears as I used to at home, and today I could write as composedly while the rebels was throwing shell into our camp as I used to when fifty miles from them. But don't call me a hard hearted wretch for my feelings for the living is just as warm as ever. But enough of this.

On the 4th of this month the rebels gave us notice to leave here in twelve hours or take the consequences. We chose the latter so accordingly on the 5th about 11 o'clock, they began operations. They commenced firing on us from three different points. They had one forty-two pounder that made a great deal of noise but done but little damage. They continued firing until late in the evening. But finding that we would neither run nor scare, they gave it up. Since then there has been more or less firing every day. Our guns replying steadily. We are every day making this place stronger, and it they let us alone a few days longer it will cost them more than it is worth to get it. There is a rumor here that they had a fight among themselves on the day they shelled us, but whether true or not I can't tell. It was said that Bragg ordered an assault on this place and some of his men refused to obey and on using force they resisted. It is said that their little fight caused the loss of five hundred men. There is something going on with them today. We can't see their fires. Last night they had hundreds of fires kindled, but I will drop the subject.

I have had one letter from Ill's since I came here. All was well and how sincerely I hope this missive will find my loving wife and child enjoying good health. Mary, if your letters contained nothing more than we are well, I would hail them [with] joy, but my paper is out and I must tell you about my washing this afternoon. You see I have but one pair of pants and having occasion to wash them, I took them off, tied my oil blanket around my waist and went at it. Now guess what kind of an appearance I made?

My warmest love to you and Ella and respects to all. Good bye.
Mc. Montgomery to Mary Montgomery
Direct to Chattanooga.

Despite his attempt in the final paragraph of the letter to lighten the mood, it did nothing to allay Mary's fears. She had never before felt such sadness. How much this awful war had changed her husband! Would he be the same thoughtful, caring man that she loved or would he forever be overwhelmed by the horrors he had witnessed? She longed for his return and prayed for the day when the killing would stop and life would again return to the ordinary routine that she had once found so dull.

Conditions continued to worsen for the Union troops under siege in Chattanooga and clearly, not only was it impossible to bring food supplies into the city, but also mail delivery was hampered. Nonetheless, Sergeant Montgomery's letter of October 16 was less ominous in tone than his last. He was pleased to report that gubernatorial elections recently held in the camp proved that the soldiers were completely loyal to the Union and that Clement Vallandigham, the notorious "Copperhead" opponent of the war, did not receive support from the regiment.

Mary Ann smiled and shook her head at his suggestion that the election was probably not of as much interest to her as it was to the

men. How typical of men to assume that she would have no interest
in an election just because she was prohibited from voting in it. But
now was not the time to take offense at the remark.

Chattanooga, Tenn, Oct. 16th 1863

Dear Wife. I have waited long and patiently for a letter from you
but having rec'd none, I have come to the conclusion that my letters have not reached you. I shall write, however, under the suppo-
sition that you have and will not pretend to recount what has
befell me again until I am answered by you that you have not
heard from me since the battle. I have written at least four letters
since that time and have not yet received an answer from any of
them. But I shall still continue to write feeling sure that either my
letters have not reached you or else your letters have failed to
reach me. I do not complain Dear, for I feel sure you will not
neglect to write if you know where I am. We have had hard times
since we came here and there is no likelihood of its being much
easier for some time to come.

I am almost dry this morning for the first time for four days. During that time it has rained almost without intermission both day
and night and still the weather looks unsettled. Our men is on
duty most all of the time, but I am getting along much easier than
I have been before. I am acting orderly sergeant and that relieves
me from all guard and picket duty. My work although confining is
not hard and I am likely to fill the place [for] sometime to come,
perhaps the rest of my time in service. We are here in fair view of
the enemy and our pickets are posted within talking distance of
them, but by mutual agreement, there is no firing from either side.
How it will end, I know not.

We held election here last Tuesday. You can tell neighbor John
Kenerd [a supporter of Vallandigham] of that. In our company
Vallandinham got nary vote and only three in the reg't. We have
heard since that he was beat 30,000 without the soldiers' vote, but
I don't suppose you feel as much interested in the election as I do
so I will say no more about it. When you write, tell me how many
letters you have received from me since the 15th of last month. I
believe the last one I got from you was dated Sep. 10th. Write soon
and tell me if you have heard from George lately. James and I are
both well. James has been having the ague but he has got it broke.
I hope, Dear Mary, this will find you and my little Ella in good

health. I shall wait anxiously for word from you Give my love to mother and my respects to all of my friends that may inquire. My heart's devotion to you and Ella. This from your absent but loving husband.
Mc to Mary Montgomery
Direct to 33rd O.V.I. Chattanooga, Tenn.

Rebel forces continued to send daily rounds of artillery down upon the city from their fortified locations on Lookout Mountain and Missionary Ridge. As Union wagons attempted to deliver much needed supplies to the Federal troops, they were hampered by Confederate raids and by roads, which due to the continuous rain eventually became impassable. President Lincoln, realizing the seriousness of the situation, decided to once again reorganize his troops. On October 17, 1863, the president sent Maj. Gen. Ulysses S. Grant to command the Military Division of the Mississippi, which included the Departments of the Ohio, the Cumberland and the Tennessee.

## Concerns from Illinois

In late October, McLain's sister-in-law, Abigail, after reading news accounts from the bloody battle at Chickamauga, Georgia, and not having received letters from him, expressed concern regarding his welfare.

Oct. 20 1863
My Dear Brother
I received a letter from you two weeks ago today and I also received one last July which I answered immediately and directed to camp near Battle Creek, Alabama, as you stated for me to in yours, but it seems that you never got it. That I cannot account for but the last one I have not answered till now for I have been waiting for John to write for he said he would too but he is so slow I will not wait any longer for him. So here goes.

In the first place we feel a good deal worried about you since the battle for as near as we can learn you was in it and as Delorain was in the battle at Corinth and came out all right as he says, we now feel anxious about you.

We are all pretty well, but Mr. Janes. He is bothered a good deal with the asthma and is rather worse tonight than usual. John's folks are all well and Newton is quite well though his wife has a young daughter one week old. Elijah's folks are or was all well the last I heard. James Burke [Company H Ninety-ninth Illinois Volunteer Infantry] has (like all the rest of the sensible fellows) joined the northern legion and gone to the wars. Bully for him. I think I hear you say.

Well, brother McLain, I think we can boast a little of our little Walnut. She has sent out some seventy odd soldiers. There is but two single men left. I will tell you their names. Isaac Kelley and Arthur Martin. They are all the young men that are fit to go to war that are left. Del feels very anxious about you. He says since you have gone to war, he thinks more of you than ever. I got a letter from Sharon Margrave a short time ago. He and his brother, Frank are in the army. The old lady is dead and the old Man is poor. The girls have to work out for a living. Father is still in Nevada Territory. He is doing pretty well.

Eliza's man [Henry H. Williams, Company B, Sixty-fourth Illinois Volunteer infantry, "Yates Sharpshooters"] has got his discharge from the army and has come home. The old man Flanderberg is dead. He died in the army at Corinth. There has been a good many deaths and a good many marriages, to say nothing of the births since you left, but I will not try to add them up on this small sheet of paper. I am still living with Mr. Janes folks and we are all making molasses. This fall, I got letters from Del every week and some times twice a week. He is or was, when he wrote last, in Corinth. I will tell you how to write to him so that you can and I want you to. I told him how to write to you in my last letter, for he wrote for me too. This is how Mr. T.D. Montgomery, Company B, 1st battalion of Yates Sharp Shooters, Corinth, Mississippi.

Now Mc, it is getting late and I must stop writing for the time. We all send our love to you and you will please send some of it to you wife for goodness sake, Mc. Did she ever see that wild letter I wrote you. If she did you must excuse it to her. Tell her I am not very smart and the best and am given to spells and that you think I must have had one then. Give my love to that soldier brother of yours that is with you. I believe you call him James. Sister Albina says if you don't write something to her next time you write, she will box your ears the first time she gets a chance. Oh, where did you get that big sheet of paper you wrote to me on. I wish this was like it for I ain't said half enough. Write as soon as you get this. Excuse my mistakes and accept of a sisters love to a soldier.

Abigail A. Montgomery.

At Chattanooga, Union troops continued to suffer from the lack of food and supplies and seemed near starvation. It was not until October 26, that General Grant's chief engineer, Brig. Gen. William "Baldy" Smith devised a plan to reopen the Tennessee River and resume transportation of supplies to the city. Later accounts from men of the Thirty-third were filled with the grim details of days and weeks of hunger. The fact that they were cut off from the outside world made it impossible to get letters out of or into Chattanooga. Perhaps this was the motivation for Sergeant Montgomery's decision on October 30, 1863, to begin a journal of his daily activities. The entries are brief with accounts of weather conditions and references to continued artillery fire. Only a few selected entries are provided here and are identified as journal entries by the letters J.E.

J.E. Chattanooga, Tennessee, November 2 1863
On reserve picket post two miles from town. Weather warm. Looks like rain. Rebels fired on our post with a piece of artillery on Lookout Mountain.

Chattanooga, Tenn, Nov. 4, 1863
Dear wife. Your welcome letter of the 24th was received today. Yes, and now I have to stop writing to read another that has just come bearing date Oct. 20th. Well, dear Mary, I can answer both at once. I am happy to hear that you and Ella is well and I am glad that I can say the same for myself. James has been absent from the regiment more than two weeks. He was detailed to go to Stevenson as guard for a provision train and has not yet returned though I expect he is faring better than he would if he were here for he is where there [is] plenty to eat, but it is scarce enough here.

The Lord knows it is now 3 o'clock P.M. and I have had nothing to eat since yesterday evening and I ate but one meal yesterday. We have been on less than half rations for more than two weeks. For a while, I bought bread from the bakery, but now it can't be had. Money is of no use for if I had my pockets full I would not know where to buy my dinner. But this sounds too much like complaining. I must quit it for I have much to be thankful for.

My health is uncommonly good and my heart is stout as ever. I can do and endure so long as a vestige of hope for the Union remains, but we have fair prospects of better times. I think this evening we will have plenty to eat. From where I set now I can look out and see the rebel tents by hundreds. When we go on picket only a small stream divides our picket line from theirs. How long this state of things will last is more than I can tell. We are comfortably situated here on a high hill which gives us a fair view of the town and almost the entire encampment of our Army and also a good portion of the enemy's. We have more or less cannonading every day. The rebels have a battery on Lookout Mountain from which they give us a few shells regularly each day. I have become so accustomed to it that I scarce every go out of my tent to see where the shells strike. The 18th Ohio battery makes a business of replying, but for all the damage that is done, I think they would both do well to stop. If we do no more damage than they, I am sure it don't pay us. You can tell Jess that he had better make his molasses for if he comes here to fight for them he will find them scarce enough.

I am glad that Ohio has so well redeemed herself in the last election for we was getting rather a bad name among her sister states. I wish I could be at home for a while now. I think I could tell every traitor by his long face, but a truce to politics and war news. I am now looking forward to the time when it will not be necessary for me to write letters to you. My time is slowly but surely coming to a close and then I hope I shall never be so far separated from you as to make it necessary for me to write. I got a letter a few days since from Dell and Abigail. They were well and all of the rest was well. Abigail sends her love to you and says kiss Ella for her. Give my respects to neighbor Kennedy. My love to mother retaining, My heart's warmest affection for yourself and Ella. Write often. Direct as before. Your affectionate husband, Mc. Montgomery to Mary Montgomery.

J.E.: Chattanooga, November 9th, The day is clear and cold with a sharp cutting breeze from the north. The rebels on Lookout Mountain have been unusually quiet today. I think yesterday evening's work made them sick of shelling pickets. A few shots from our guns on Moccasin Mt. is all the firing that has been done today.

J.E. Nov. 12th. Clear, frosty morning still continues but the days are pleasant. About 12 Noon there was quite a number of shots came from Lookout and was promptly answered from the point. The firing lasted for about an hour.

J.E. Chattanooga, Tenn. Nov. 18th, 1863 The weather today is warm and cloudy. Everything is quiet in front. Shots from Lookout is less frequent than common. Considerable numbers of deserters come through our lines daily.

J.E. Sunday, 22nd of November '63 We was relieved this morning. The weather is clear and cold. Several shots has been fired today from Fort Wood and the guns on the point have been very busy all the afternoon. There appears to be a grand move afoot, but what it is, is hard to tell. We are ordered to be ready to march tomorrow at 6 A.M.

J.E. Chattanooga, 23rd Nov. 11 o'clock A.M. the orders to march this morning was countermanded. We are under orders to be ready to move at a moments notice. A few shots from our batteries on the point is all that has occurred in the way of hostilities up to this time.

## Battles of Lookout Mountain and Missionary Ridge.

J.E. Nov. 24th, 6 A.M. After dark last night our brigade moved to the left and formed in line. We were still here at 9 P.M. About one o'clock this afternoon we moved in the direction of Lookout Mountain where our men have been pressing the rebels closely since about 11 A.M. We crossed Chattanooga Creek and climbed Lookout Mountain just at dark. Although there is a heavy fog hanging over us sharp skirmishing still continues.

The Thirty-third Ohio had been ordered to relieve an Iowa regiment along the cliffs surrounding the top of the mountain. Late that night, Rebel forces relinquished their hold on Lookout Mountain. At about 11:00 p.m., to conceal their withdrawal, they began shelling the Union troops who had been steadily advancing throughout the day. Losses suffered by the Thirty-third included one man killed and two wounded.

Early the next morning, it was discovered that the enemy troops had abandoned their position. Men from the Eighth Kentucky hoisted the National colors as evidence to the Union troops below that the Union forces had prevailed. The men were jubilant, but after only a few hours of rest and celebration, they were called into formation and about 11:00 a.m. they were ordered to march toward Missionary Ridge where they would again engage the rebels.

> J.E. Nov. 25th This morning finds us in full possession of Lookout. About noon we came down from the mountain, crossed Chattanooga Creek and had the satisfaction [of] seeing a steam boat come around the point, thus showing free navigation. After a short rest, we moved in the direction of Missionary Ridge. About 5 in the evening, we took possession of the rebel rifle pits at the foot of the ridge. We then charged up the hill. In making the charge I received a wound in the left groin, thus ending my fighting. I had, however the satisfaction of seeing our flag on top of the ridge before I left the field.

Sergeant Montgomery was among the twenty-seven men from the Thirty-third wounded that day. The regiment also suffered six men who were killed. Due to the severity of his wound, Sergeant Montgomery was confined to the hospital in Chattanooga, while the regiment continued south to Ringgold, Georgia, in pursuit of General Bragg's troops.

> J.E. Nov. 26h Today I am in the Hospital. I am getting along much better than I had any reason to hope for. The news from the front is very encouraging. Large numbers of farmers have been coming in all day.

> J.E. Chattanooga, Nov. 27th I have heard but little from the front today. Reports that have come in, however, is very cheering. The enemy is reported in full retreat closely pursued by our troops. The weather is warm and cloudy. Looks like rain.

At Ringgold, Union troops found the Confederate forces entrenched upon a ridge. The men of the Thirty-third witnessed the advance of the Thirty-eighth Indiana as they advanced up the ridge. The engagement lasted only about a half hour before the Union forces gained control of the ridge, without the loss of a man. On Sunday, November 29, the brigade returned to their camp in Chattanooga.

Sergeant Montgomery's entries continued from Hospital Number 3, Chattanooga, Tennessee, while his wound was improving. Although he was becoming restless at being confined, he was feeling well enough to compose a brief letter to Mary. It was the first he had written since early November.

Reports from local newspapers at home as well as letters from other men to their families had filled the Montgomery household with fear. Mary tried hard to hold on to her faith and not to fill her head with all manner of disasters that might have befallen her husband. But her efforts were futile and sleepless nights seemed to drag on forever. When a letter finally arrived, she took a deep breath before opening it and gave a silent prayer that her husband was unharmed. But a dark foreboding fear caused her hands to shake as she began to read.

December 1, 1863

Dear wife. You will have to put up with a short letter this time because I am not able to write a long one. I received a letter from you some [time] since, but have not had a chance to answer it until after the fight. I was wounded the second day of the fight in the evening. That was November the 25th. I might have written a line the next day, but I could give no account of James so I resolved to wait until I heard from him. But the fight is over and James has again escaped unharmed. My strength will not permit me to enter into details now but when I get a little better, I will write you a long letter. My wound is severe but not dangerous and already looks better. Enclosed you will find an order on Ben & Mites for seventeen dollars. I want you to take it and get necessaries for you and Ella for the present winter and don't Dear Mary give yourself any trouble about me. I am well cared for and am doing well. My love to mother and respects to all. Yours, dear Mary, while life lasts. Mc Montgomery to Mary Montgomery.

P.S. My wound is in the left groin.
Direct to Gen. Johnson's Division, Hospital No. 3, Chattanooga, Tenn.

In his entries for December 2 through December 4, Sergeant Montgomery briefly commented that the weather was warm and pleasant and that everything was quiet. By December 5, rain and cooler weather had arrived, and Sergeant Montgomery was making preparations to leave the hospital at Chattanooga and made no entries in his journal until December 17.

> J.E. Dec. 17th Walked one miles and a half. Went on board of the steamer *Paint Rock* at 22 A.M. left Chattanooga at 5 P.M. Arrived at Bridgeport at 12 o'clock at night. Weather very cold.

> J.E. Bridgeport, Dec. 18th This morning I find myself at the field hospital at Bridgeport, Ala. With a promise of transportation this evening for Nashville, Ten. Weather clear and cold.

As with many things in the military, delays occurred and for the next three days he impatiently awaited transport that finally commenced on December 22.

> J.E. Bridgeport, Ala. Dec. 22nd. Got on the cars at 9 A.M. it is now 1 ½ o'clock and we are still here. We got off at 4 P.M. arrived at Stevenson about 5 ½ P.M. After some delay we started for Nashville. Arrived at Dechard Station about midnight, where, on account of an accident to the (?) train, we were obliged to lay by until morning. The accident proved to be quite serious. Several lives were lost and several badly bruised.

> J.E. Dec. 23rd. After a cold and tedious ride in a box car, arrived at Nashville about 9 P.M and was taken to the Cumberland Hospital.

By Christmas day, Sergeant Montgomery was well enough for a holiday excursion into the city.

> J.E. Dec. 25 Christmas I make this entry 11 P.M. I have passed the day very pleasantly. I have been in the city since 2 PM. Went to the theater. I shall pass the night at Hospital No. 3. It has been raining since 9 P.M.

The rain continued for the next four days and contributed to his discomfort. On New Year's Eve, perhaps to mark the end of a costly and remarkable year, Sergeant Montgomery took time to prepare a more lengthy entry into his journal.

J.E. Cumberland Hospital, Dec. 31st. This is the last day of the old year. It has been marked with events that live in our Nation's history until time shall be no more. The last of the old year is a sad prototype of the political storms that has raged since the year began. The last days of the preceding was made hideous by the storm of battle and tonight the storm fiend appears to have broken loose in all his fury. The wind blows a perfect hurricane and the snow comes in fitful gusts making it cold and cheerless enough.

The year of 1863 ended for Mary and Ella with the same empty feeling with which it began. She had not seen her husband for nearly two years and it appeared that the war was no nearer to ending than the year before. The losses kept mounting and Mary's fears for her husband's safety grew daily.

# CHAPTER 12

# *A Much Needed Furlough*
# *1864*

---

## News from Illinois

For Sergeant Montgomery, the New Year would begin much the same as the previous had ended. He was in the hospital, lonely, and with no real anticipation that the war would soon be ended. That knowledge, coupled with the cold rainy weather that soon changed to snow did little to improve his spirits.

> J.E. Nashville, Tenn. January first, 1864 The New Year has brought cold weather with it. There is nothing going on to excite attention, but strange events are to unfold themselves in the future. Twelve months is more than human laws can tell but let us hope that another new year may find our nation at rest and purer from the tribulation through which it has passed.

After spending another week in the hospital, McLain would have been cheered by any news from family; however, as evidence of the unreliable and very slow mail delivery, the following two letters from his relatives in Illinois were not received by Sergeant Montgomery until mid April. They are included here to be consistent with the chronology of events.

Greenville
Jan. 7th '64

Dear Brother,

We received yours of the 1st of Dec. day before yesterday and was happy to hear that you was recoverin from your wound. We got your other letter that you wrote after the battle. We answered it and sent it to Chattanooga, so if you are at home you won't get it and I will have to give you the news over again.

To begin with Brother Newton has enlisted and gone off to the Army along with Bill Brewer. Bill got about thirty recruits and left. I don't know whether he will get a commission or not.

Thirty-two-year-old Bill Brewer, an Indiana native, indeed convinced a group of young men from Bureau County to go to Peoria County to enlist in the Union army; however, Del's estimate seems exaggerated since only nine men from Bureau County, actually enlisted. On December 30, 1863, Bill Brewer and the following men enlisted as privates in Company I, Thirty-first Illinois Infantry.

| Name | Age | Remarks |
|------|-----|---------|
| Bill Brewer | 32 | promoted to 2nd Lt. June 11, 1864, of Co. I, 64th Illinois Infantry |
| William A. Burke | 18 | promoted to corporal Jan. 1865 |
| James B. Green | 18 | killed near Atlanta, July 22, 1864 |
| Charles A. Kelly | 18 | died of disease, Aug. 27, 1864 |
| Charles A. Koons | 22 | mustered out July 19, 1865 |
| Zina C. Knights | 19 | mustered out July 19, 1865 |
| Isaac N. Montgomery | 35 | mustered out on cert. of disability |
| James W. Perdew | 20 | died of disease Aug. 8, 1864 |
| Andrew Peterson | 45 | mustered out on cert. of disability |

Brother Del also included news of several local men from Company I of the Ninety-third Illinois Infantry. Nearly every man in Company I was from Bureau County and the regiment, like Sergeant Montgomery's had fought in the battles of Chickamauga, Lookout Mountain, and Missionary Ridge. In his letter he refers to the battle of

Missionary Ridge, November 25, 1863.

Nathan Meek mentioned below was the son of Richard Meek and grandson of Samuel Meek who were two of the members of the posse of men who had searched for and found the body of young Salina Montgomery in 1849. Nathan's brother, William Meek, also served in this regiment.

> Nathan Meek is at home on furlough. He got a shot in the left arm about the same time you was wounded. Cornelius Siger [Segar] and Dan Pomphrey deserted in time of the Battle and haven't been heard of since. Robert Sample was killed dead on the field. That is all the news of the battle that I can give you seeing that you was there and took part in the fray.

Official records indicate that Pvt. Cornelius Segar did, indeed, desert on November 24, 1863, near Chattanooga, Tennessee. However, there is no official record that Pvt. Daniel Pomphrey deserted. He served for the duration of the war and on June 18, 1865, he was transferred to Company K of the Fortieth Illinois Infantry.

> The local news don't amount to much. All that there is about it is that the weather is rather cool. We have had quite a cool snap. It commenced snowing the day before New Years from the North West. It was strong all day and night to well you know how it blows here when it gets started. Well, it got cold then colder and finally most infernal cold. Yes colder than that cattle and horses froze to death. Hogs, chickens, turkeys and the quails all lay dead in the snow. You can scarcely see a bird of any description left alive. We had about 25 quails that stayed around the house with the chickens. They are all dead. John lost one cow and one hog. Richard Meek lost 5 head of cattle and one horse and others lost in proportion. And it is very cold yet. The oldest inhabitants never saw anything equal to it. All we do is to get coal and keep fires and play Seven Up and bad luck to it. Our cards are about gone up. Haven't you a spare deck that you could lend a feller to kill time with.

> We can't hunt or trap any. I tried it one day this week. Speared four [musk]rats, frosted the ends of my fingers, went home and quit. We have sold our mink at a fair price. We had 21 and sold for three fifty a piece. We haven't sold any [musk]rats yet. We have

near two thousand. Deacon Janes is trapping some and has had good success. Frank and Newton Bard and I intended to go to Vermillian to try it awhile but the weather is so cold we can't go . While I think of it, I will just [confide] to you it is rather cool here.

Tell Mary that Abbi sends her love to her. Our little Mary says she wishes her Uncle Mc would come home from the war. N. Bard sends his respects to you. When you write again to us direct your letters to New Bedford. It is nearer for us to go to Tailhalt than it is to Walnut. Write as often as you can to either one of us and you will get an answer. The reason that I haven't wrote oftener of late is that I have been away with my traps the most of the time and Abigail had all the writing to do. Well, I haven't much more to say. One thing more Old Pomphrey is dead. He was killed by a tree falling on him. Our folks and connections are all well. Write as soon as you get this.
Your affectionate Brother,
Del
To McLain Montgomerie

A few days after the receipt of the letter from Del, McLain received another from Del's wife, Abigail, in which she expressed her pleasure with his decision not to reenlist for another tour of duty.

Greenville, Ill.
February 15, 1864

My Dear Brother and sister
We received your letter of the 21st but we did not get it as soon as we should for we could not cross the river. We are all well and very glad to hear you are at home and getting along so well, and I am glad you have not enlisted in the veteran Corps. I think you have served your country well and if you are spared for the next five months you should serve your family instead. The boys from here have most all reenlisted and are at home on furlough. We are a having the finest weather now I most ever seen for the time of the year. It almost gives me the spring fever. We got a letter from Samantha last week. She is at father's now. They are keeping house. Francina McNitt has a young baby, another boy. They were all well. my sister Eliza lost a little girl two weeks ago. It was two weeks old. She has lost three children now and has two living.

The men have not sold their fur yet. They have over two thousand muskrats and considerable other fur, but it is not high as it is sometimes. They have quit trapping now for a while and are chopping and splitting rails. Mr. Janes was down a little while ago. His folks are all well. Now Brother Mc about that of yours. You say she is the smartest Montgomery you ever saw. Well that ain't saying much for her, but you have not seen my Molly yet or you would not talk so. Why Mc, she can climb any tree in this grove, ride horseback straddle, go a fishing and catch fish . . . and other accomplishments too numerous to mention for a young lady. For you see, I calculate to make a lady of her. In fact, she is almost a lady now. Mc, I declare I don't know what to write that would interest you. I hope when you are discharged from the army, you will come to Illinois to live so we can see one another some times. It is nearly six years since we have seen you. Sister Mary, I wish you would write to me some times. If I am not personally acquainted with you, I feel an interest in your welfare and a letter from you would be welcome. We all send our love to you.

Write soon
Your brother and sister
A.A. and T. D. Montgomerie

## Finally, a Furlough Home

Shortly after this, Sergeant Montgomery was given a furlough home, where he occupied some of his time in carving a crutch for himself. On it, he proudly inscribed the names of the several battles in which he had fought.

There are no further journal entries until his departure from Wheelersburg to journey back to the regiment in early March; however, he received this letter from Cpl. Samuel Roxby, Company A, Thirty-third Ohio.

Feb. 18th -64
Chattanooga, Tenn.
Sir:
I received your letter. I was glad to hear that you are getting well again. Those of us that did not reenlist have been transferred to the 94th Ohio. We are camped at present in front of Fort Wood. I am

in Company F. James is in company D. James is sick in hospital. He is getting better. He is well taken care of. You need not be alarmed about him. I do not think there is any danger. I was over to see him today. He says he feels a good deal better. I have no news to tell you except that we have to drill four hours a day. I suppose you know how I like it. I feel disgusted with everything belonging to the army. Time drags heavy with me. I want to be free once more. I am sick of being a slave to others. Between pickett and fort work, and drill we have little time to ourselves. I shall go over to see James as often as I can. He has not read the letter you sent him. He says he cannot see to read it yet. I shall send you word how he is getting along whenever I have time to see him. I want you to write as soon as you get this and let me know all about the old Reg.'t and all the other news you hear of. Write soon.

Yours Respectfully

Samuel Roxby.

P.S. Direct to the 94th Ohio Vol. Co. F. Chattanooga

## Return to Duty

On March 7, 1864, McLain left his wife and daughter at 9:00 a.m. expecting to catch a ride at Portsmouth on the steamer *Bostona* for Cincinnati. Unfortunately, the steamer had already departed by the time he arrived at noon and he went to the Biggs House to spend the remainder of the day until the departure of the next steamer. At midnight, he boarded the *F. E. Dumont*, and arrived in Cincinnati at seven o'clock the next morning. From there he left for Camp Dennison where he arrived at six o'clock that evening. Once again, his journal entries included sparse details and brief weather descriptions. His entry for March 9 indicated that he had written to Mary.

The next two days were cold and rainy and he occupied his time by writing to Wheelersburg neighbors W. B. McNeal and Isaac N. Winkler and to his wife, Mary Ann.

Camp Dennison, March 12th, 64

Dear wife. As I am still here and nothing to do I might just as well write you a few lines as not. It is true I have nothing new to write but I have just received a letter from Dell & Abby. I wish to send it home and I thought I would just send a few lines with it. We have been ordered to Chattanooga but the colonel went to Columbus yesterday evening to try to get longer time. What the result will be I can't tell but I expect we will remain here for some time yet. If you have any letters from Ill's or from Roxby please send them along and if you have heard from James let me know how he is. I was in hopes I would have been near him before this but it is even doubtful if we go there at all now. If the Col. gets longer time we may be sent to Virginia. According to the papers Lieutenant General U.S. Grant says we must take the rebel capitol before we penetrate farther into the Confederacy. If that rumor is true, it will give our army at Chattanooga some rest. Since I have been here, I have heard that all men that volunteered during the summer & fall of 1861 would be mustered out of the service in June. It may and it may not be [the] case. At the best, I cannot count on getting home before my time is out.

Direct all of your letters in care of Col. O. F. Moore and then if I should leave they will be sure to follow give my love to mother and my respects to father and kiss Ella for me and write. Ever yours. Mc. Montgomery to Mary.

The next three days at Camp Dennison continued cold and blustery with heavy snow squalls. On March 15, Sergeant Montgomery wrote to his Scioto County cousin Hannah Montgomery, daughter of his uncle Abraham, and also to his beloved Mary with promises that he would not reenlist and a reassurance that he would return to her and little Ella.

Camp Dennison, Ohio March 15th '64

Dear Wife. I received your kind letter this morning and I was glad to hear that my dear Mary and my darling Ella was well. You beg of me not to reenlist and ask me to remember you and Ella. Do you suppose that I could ever forget you after so pleasant a stay at home as I had. No, I enjoyed myself too well ever to forget for one moment; and I will return to those pleasures again just as soon as it is possible for me to do so. Even if there were nothing to attract me at home, I do not think that I should reenlist for I am heartily sick and tired of the company that I am forced to associate with. So you need have no fears on that score.

Perhaps it is human nature to voice previously unspoken words of discontent when a final decision has been made to remove oneself from a set of undesirable circumstances. Whatever the motivation, Sergeant Montgomery did not hesitate to tell Mary about the unacceptable situation he encountered at Camp Dennison while waiting to return to the regiment and the end of his enlistment.

Never in my life have I passed a week in good health and enjoyed myself so little as in the week past. We have no order whatever. Everything is confusion and to get an hour of quiet conversation is among the impossibilities. And the noise generally kept up until midnight and after. But I have a good messmate, one of your old acquaintances. It is Robert Gibbins [sergeant, Company A]. We have a comfortable place to stay, but how long we will remain here is hard to tell. The 53rd left here this morning. The small pox is in camp but I don't think I have any cause to fear it. I was vaccinated when I first came here but it took no effect on me.

Now dear Mary, I shall expect an answer to this for I want you to write half as many letters at least as I do. I suppose you have got my second letter before this time. You need send no more paper while I remain here for I have as many sheets of paper as I have envelopes, and I cannot take care of more very well and then this is too big while I stay here for there is no news to fill it. It is now nine o'clock and we are going to have inspection at half past ten so I will have to stop writing and go to work on al old rusty gun. Give my love to mother. My respects to father and remember that my heart's warmest affections is yours and Ella's. From your affectionate husband Mc. Montgomery to Mary Montgomery
P. S. direct hereafter in care of Col. O. F. Moore, and then if I should leave, your letter will be sure to follow. Mc. M.

Finally on March 16, the men left Camp Dennison at two o'clock in the afternoon and arrived in Cincinnati at six o'clock that evening. They immediately were housed in the barracks located on Fifth Street. The following day they departed from the landing at Cincinnati at two o'clock onboard the steamer *General Lytle* and arrived in Louisville, Kentucky, later that night. He remained in Louisville for the next two days during which time he paid a visit to Sgt. John W. Schencks, Company F of the Thirty-third.

On March 19 they left Louisville by train bound for Nashville, Tennessee, and arrived there about four o'clock in the early morning at Barracks Number 2, from which place he wrote to Mary.

Nashville, Tennessee, Monday, March 20th 1864

Dear Wife. My conveniences for writing is very poor but I will try and pen a few lines to let you know where I am. We left Camp Dennison on the 16th. Went as far as Cincinnati, stayed over night and until three o'clock the next day. We then left for Louisville on board the steamer *General Lytle*. Arrived in Louisville about 2 o'clock next morning where we remained [until] 3 o'clock the next day (19th). We then left on the cars for this place and arrived here this morning about 4 o'clock. It is more than likely that we will remain here for several days. The 53rd Regt. is here. I have been with Morell McNeal [Capt. Morrell G. McNeal, 53rd Ohio Infantry] all day. They expect to leave tomorrow.

I have not been very well since I left camp Dennison, but I guess it is no more than a bad cold and the want of sleep; the regiment has been drunk ever since we left camp. In fact they never been sober since we got together so I have not had a good night's sleep since I left home. Last night we had a very disagreeable ride on the cars. It was cold and we had no fire so sleep was out of the question. So under the circumstances you must excuse me if my letter is not very long or interesting.

You may tell mother that if I don't get to Chattanooga soon, James's apples will all be rotten, but I will keep them as long as I can. If I could carry them without bruising them the would keep much longer, but that is impossible. But I will have to quit for the present. I feel too bad to write but you need give yourself no trouble on my account for just as soon as I get a day or two's rest, I will be all right again. Give my love to mother. Tell Ella that Pa will come as soon as he can. Kiss her for me. God bye from your affectionate Husband
Mc. Montgomery to Mary Montgomery

In his journal, McLain noted that for the next four days he occupied his time by visiting friends who were confined at the Cumberland Hospital and in writing letters. On March 24 the majority of the regiment left Nashville, but Sergeant Montgomery, along with nineteen other men, were left behind to take care of the baggage. In all probability these were chosen since they had proven that they were reliable and sober. A welcome bonus was the fact that he was free to go to the theater later that evening. In the following letter to Mary, he did not mention his theater excursion.

Nashville Tenne. March 24th '64

Dear Wife. Thinking that a letter from me would be welcome at any time and having a good opportunity [to] write, I thought I could not improve the time better than in writing to you. It is true I have nothing of special interest to write but if I should wait for items of interest, you would have to wait for some time for a letter.

The regiment left this morning for Chattanooga. They are going to march through. I am left with the baggage and will go through on the cars when I do go, but when that will be is more than I can tell. We may leave this afternoon and we may be here for three or four days. I am I charge of twenty men. We have got a room to ourselves so we are comfortable situated. Our meals is furnished at the Barracks so we have nothing to do but make ourselves as comfortable as possible. I could enjoy my self tolerable well if I was in good health, but I am not. But you need not be uneasy for it is nothing but a bad cold and in a few days I will be well again. Now Dear Mary, I want to know if you have heard anything from James or have you got any letters from Ills. If you have please send them to me. You can direct to this place until I tell you different.

Confidential [section missing]
Give my love to mother. Remember that my heart's warmest affections is yours. Give Ella a dozen kisses and tell [her] they are for Pa.

———

March 25th, 186[4]

Dearest wife. I wrote to you yesterday and I did not expect to write so soon, but I received a letter from you this morning and as I am about to leave here, I thought I would write a few lines for fear I would not have an opportunity of writing again for sometime.

Yesterday I told you I was not very well. Today I am better but still I am not able to stand the fatigues of a long march. Neither do I intend to try. We that are left behind will probably start for Chattanooga this afternoon. If we do we will get there at least two weeks ahead of the regiment.

Now I will tell you confidentially that I do not intend doing much duty this summer for this reason. We have no commissioned officer with us that cares any thing about the company and I don't care whether I stay with the company or not. I intend to put in the remainder of my time as easy as possible, but this you must tell to no one. These few lines I have written in a hurry and under disadvantage. It is raining hard and the room is crowded and I have nothing to write on but my knee, so you must excuse bad spelling and all mistakes. With my love to mother and my Blessing for you and Ella. I close hoping to hear from you soon.
Your loving husband
Mc Montgomery to Mary Montgomery

The following day, McLain and the other men who had been left behind departed Nashville by train at four thirty for Chattanooga. As they passed through Murfreesboro, Tennessee, just after dark they were aware that the regiment was still there. He arrived in Chattanooga the following day at noon and acquired accommodations at the Soldiers Home. On March 28, they left the Soldiers Home and took up quarters in a church on the east side of town and later in the evening moved to the post barracks.

On Wednesday, March 30, McLain and the others left Chattanooga at nine o'clock in the morning and arrived at Greysville, Georgia, at eleven o'clock that night and occupied the place they assumed would be their future camp and settled down to await the arrival of the rest of the regiment.

## Into Georgia with General Sherman

Greysville, Georgia
March 31st 1864

Dear Wife. I have arrived at my destination safe and in better health than I expected. I have not seen James yet and I cannot find out where he is but I think he is at Chattanooga. I am going down there tomorrow to try and find him. I got here yesterday about ten o'clock and have not had a chance to look around much. I found my old friend Roxby here. He has not heard from James since he wrote that letter that I got while I was at home. The hospital that James was in was broken up and the Brigade left and came here and they don't know where James was sent to.

You can tell mother that I have came up with that letter that I wrote for her on the 2nd of this month. James never got it. It came to the reg't but they did [not] know where to send it, but you can tell her that I will do the best I can to find him tomorrow.

*James Montgomery*

We are about 18 miles S.E. from Chattanooga. We are just over the state line. Five minutes walk will take us back into Tenn. When you write to me, direct your letter to Chattanooga, Co., Reg't & Div. same as before. The Reg't will not be here for a week yet, but I will not write more this time for I expect to write again just as soon as I find where James is. Give my love to mother and write soon and may the Blessing of Heaven abide with you and my dear child is the prayer of your devoted husband.
Mc Montgomery
Mary Montgomery

On April 1, McLain, having learned of the whereabouts of James, had gone to Chattanooga to visit him and remained there until April 3 when he returned to camp where on April 5, he and Samuel Roxby put up a tent which they intended to share. On April 7, they received word that the regiment had finally arrived in Chattanooga.

In the second paragraph from his April 7, 1864, letter to Mary,

Sergeant Montgomery made a veiled and discreet inquiry regarding whether or not Mary was pregnant with their second child. He reminded her that a simple "yes" or "no" would be the only response he needed.

Greysville, Ga., April 7th '64

Dear Wife. I receive a letter from you this morning and was sorry to hear that you was unwell. How glad I will be when I can come home and tend on you when you are sick. As my time draws nearer to a close, the more impatient I get. A day is as a week used to be, a week a month and a month appears to be without end,. But where the treasure is there will the heart be also. All of my hearts best feelings is far away with you and Ella. You must, for my sake, take good care of yourself and if you need medical advice do not put it off until you are bedfast, but send at once. I suppose mother has received the letter I wrote from the hospital, but for fear it has not reached her, I will just state that I was down to Chattanooga last Friday and remained with James until Sunday. He is getting better fast, but I advised him to stay there as long as he could. He has a comfortable place to stay and good wholesome food. If you want to write to him, direct to General Field Hospital Ward B.

In confidence, when I left home I asked you for certain information which you could not give at that time. In all probability you can do so now. You remember how I told you to answer a single word is sufficient, yes or no is easily written and they will convey the intelligence I ask for as well as half a page. If you knew Dear Mary how deeply I am interested in all that is likely to affect your welfare, you would not hesitate to answer.

I rec'd a letter from Dell and Abigail a few days since. I will send the letter enclosed to you that will save me the trouble of telling you the news. [See chapter nine for these letters that were written in January and February.] Give my love to mother and kiss our little pet for me and answer this as soon as you can make it convenient.

Yours affectionately
Mc Montgomery to Mary Montgomery
Direct Chattanooga

———

Graysville, Ga., April 14th 1864

Dear wife. As I sit alone in my tent today the weather [is] too cold to enjoy life out of doors. The regiment is on picket (or at least the most of it). I very naturally grow lonesome and my thoughts turn homewards and I wonder why you do not write , but then I remember the uncertainty of the mails and think you perhaps have not rec'd my letters. At all events, I will try and be patient well knowing that your knowledge of my love will tell you how anxious I am to hear from you.

Dear Mary, when a day of quiet like this falls to us here, where such days are so few, my mind grows and rests not, until it alights on the prospects of home which each day is bringing nearer. The time since I left home seems long, yes, very long, but the time that is before me, that must elapse before I can again enjoy the pleasure of your society seems like an age. Yet must I submit and I will do so without a murmur if I can, but the time, once past and I find myself free from all restraint, nothing shall ever tempt me to leave you again. The last letter I got from you, you was unwell and oh, how anxiously have I waited for to hear from you again. At times I fear you are sick and cannot write. But I will try and be more patient. I hope there is a letter on the way for me now. Yes, it may come tonight.

Dear Mary has Ella forgot me yet? Does she ever look out of the window and ask where is pa? Oh, how I long to clasp the little [one] in my arms again and if ever the time comes when I can do so again, it will not be of my own free will that [I] leave her again. While you are waiting for me Mary watch over that child. Try to instill into her earliest understanding the principles of truth. Let example follow receipt and the result need not be feared. But deal gently with her. Speak mild to her but be firm. Never yield a point to her, but never chastise her in anger. In this way she [will] learn to obey through love rather than fear. How much better is such obedience.

But it is getting late in the evening. The mail will soon go out and if I send this I must close for this time. This leaves me in tolerable health. My mind is sad and gloomy but then I am alone and the weather is gloomy. A word from you and a few days of fine weather will make me more cheerful. I have not heard from James

since I was down to see him. I will try and go down again as soon
as I can. Give my love to mother and write soon. May Heavens
choicest blessings abide with you and Ella is the fervent prayer of
your devoted husband.
Mc Montgomery
Mary Montgomery

In the spring of 1864 there was concern in southern Ohio over the
inability of some physicians to correctly identify cases of smallpox,
especially if the case was mild. They sometimes incorrectly concluded
that the illness was chicken pox and thus failed to warn the general
population of the necessity of precaution. This may be the situation
Mary Ann reported to her husband, or possibly there was an outbreak
of influenza. Whatever the case, Sergeant Montgomery worried as
much about his wife and daughter as they did about him.

Graysville, Georgia, April 15th, 1864

Dear Wife. Yesterday I received a letter from you and although
my mind was relieved from a certain uneasiness, yet I am not satisfied. You say you are not well, but you failed to tell me what the
nature of your sickness was and you cannot wonder that I should
be uneasy when you tell me that so many are dying. I fear you are
worse off than you would have me believe. When you write again,
please tell me if there is anything serious the matter. If there is, I
will make an effort to come to you. I am not in very good health
myself at present. But there is nothing to be alarmed at. I have
been troubled with the rhumatise in the hip ever since I came here.
Yesterday the doctor put a blister on my back and today it is very
sore. (I wish the doctor had as big a one on his stern). Otherwise, I
am in good health.

You can tell mother that I had rather bad luck with a part of the
things that I brought. The apples got frozen before I left camp
Dennison and by the time I got to Nashville they was spoiled. By
the time I got here the cakes was mashed up fine enough to mix
over again. The butter and beef, tobacco and socks came through
in good order. I have not seen James since I wrote to mother. I
want to go down this week if I possibly can. We are having tolerable easy times here at present. Our duty is not hard and we have
plenty to eat and I have a very comfortable place to stay. I built a
shanty out of poles and plastered it up with mud and covered it

with my tent and then made a fire place so I can do my cooking under cover. We have had more need of the fireplace than I expected when I was making it. Day before yesterday morning we had a big frost . Indeed, we have had little else than cold weather all this month. There has been but very few days that we did not need fire. How is the weather in Ohio?

[The bottom portion of the above letter is missing.]

Apr. 18th –25th, Graysville, Georgia
Dear Wife. Having wrote two letters since I received one from you, I thought I would wait until I rec'd one before writing again, but after waiting for some time without hearing from you I have resolved to write again although I expect there is a letter on the way for me now. When you wrote last, you was unwell and I have been living in suspense ever since. And after waiting so long I fear you are sick abed and unable to write and when I think of that I almost dread to hear from home lest my fears should be realized, but a word from you confirming my fears would be but little worse that this uncertainty. I think of you all day and dream of you all night. So dearest Mary if you have not written pray write soon.

In my last letter I wrote that I was not very well being troubled with a lame back, but I am better now. We have but little to do here. We drill a little each day and go on picket about once a week. Spring has come at last and everything looks gay. I alone am sad and if I was sure that you was well I would be as well content here as I could be any where away from home. There is no news stirring that would be likely to interest you. I have not been down to see James yet nor have I heard from him. I wrote to him the day I got your last letter and sent mothers letter to him, but I have but little fear but what he is getting along very well. All he appeared to need when I saw him was rest and I advised him to stay there until he was entirely well . . . but it is nearly the hour for drill and I will have to quit for this time and I hope you will not fail to write as soon as possible. Give my love to mother. Kiss my darling Ella for me and may God bless you both. Farewell for the present.
Mc Montgomery
Mary Montgomery.

————

Graysville, Ga. Apr 28th

Dear wife. Last evening I received the long looked for letter. After devouring its contents I felt much relieved for it told of better health at home. You say you have answered all of my letters If you have either you have not got half of the letters that I have wrote or else I have not got yours for I have written more than as many again as I have received. There must be four or five letters on the route some place for one or the other of us. I write this morning not because I have anything new or interesting to write, but because our reg't is going on five days picket duty and I may not have a chance to write again until we come back. James will be left here in camp.

Now, about that money of Mathias Baccus's [resident of Ironton, Lawrence County, Ohio]. He did give me twenty dollars at Chattanooga to carry home for him, but when I got to Nashville, I got tired of carrying it and I sent it up as he directed. I saw Mathias at Louisville as I came this way, but did not have time to speak to him about it. But [it] is alright with me for I acted according to orders. If it is lost it is his loss not mine.

But I will have to wind up for the present and prepare for the five days duty. We go to Parkers Gap. It is about five miles. I will write again as soon as I come back.

I am a great deal better satisfied since you answered my questions. Now dear Mary, for my sake, take good care of yourself and Mary God bless you and protect you is the fervent prayer of him that would die to save you. Kiss my darling for me [and] give my love to mother and write often. From your devoted husband

Mc Montgomery

Mary Montgomery

**CHAPTER 13**

# *July and August 1864*

## *One Hundred Days Men*

While Sergeant Montgomery seemed fully content with the routine and uneventful days the regiment was spending in Georgia, President Lincoln and his advisors were only too keenly aware that more massive and bloody campaigns were about to begin. As the tours of duty of many of the three-year volunteers were about to end, and the costly effects of the battles of the previous year required constant replenishment of forces, drastic measures were once again required. On February 1, 1864, President Lincoln issued a call for an additional five hundred thousand volunteers. This was followed by a call on March 14 for two hundred thousand more.

Newly elected Ohio governor John Brough had handily defeated the infamous copperhead, Clement Vallandigham and had campaigned heavily with a promise to support the Union at all costs. Brough had been concerned that Ohio's southern border was vulnerable and that another raid such as the one conducted by Brig. Gen. John Hunt Morgan the previous year would jeopardize the stability and security of his state. Consequently, he personally contacted the governors of Indiana, Illinois, Iowa, and Wisconsin with a plea that they, along with Ohio, would offer to President Lincoln their promise to provide immediately a body of men who would serve for one hundred days. The rationale was that if these five states could quickly deliver eighty-five thousand men who could be sent to act as guards in rear-echelon positions, it would free up veteran troops to pursue fighting at the front. The battle cry was "One hundred days to Richmond." Lincoln solicited the opinion of Gen. Ulysses S. Grant who replied, "As a rule I would oppose accepting men for a short term, but if one hundred thousand men can be raised in the time provided . . . they might come at such a time of crisis as to be of vast importance." Accordingly, Lincoln accepted Brough's offer. The original plan called for the following number of men per state: Ohio, thirty thousand; Indiana, twenty thousand; Illinois, twenty thousand; Wisconsin, ten thousand; and Iowa, five thousand. Within sixteen days Ohio had enlisted forty regiments consisting of thirty-six thousand men. Illinois enlisted the second highest number of men with eleven regiments going into the field.

The 140th regiment was recruited from Scioto County, and two more men from the Montgomery family were among them. William Henry H. Montgomery, younger brother of Homer and Ellis Montgomery enlisted in Company E, while Mary's brother-in-law, Joseph Hopkins, husband of her sister, Sarah, enlisted in Company F. Excitement was intense as enthusiasm for a possible quick end to the war spread and newspapers and local gossip predicted a speedy and decisive victory to end the war. "One hundred days to Richmond" was the battle cry as the new recruits prepared to join the war effort.

For Mary Ann the prediction that this dreadful war would be won within one hundred days held an ominous foreboding. Past experience warned her that the outcome might not result in triumphant exaltation, but in some unimaginable disaster. She closed her eyes, took a deep breath and hugged little Ella tightly to her bosom as she said a silent prayer that her fears were unwarranted and that her beloved husband would be returning to her soon. She feared that the remaining months of her husband's service would crawl by even more slowly than the preceding three years.

## News From Illinois

For Sergeant Montgomery, news from anyone at home or from Illinois was appreciated and when he received a lengthy letter from his newlywed niece, Adaline Janes, he was pleased and somewhat surprised. Apparently Adaline had persuaded her husband, nineteen-year-old William Landers, to write to her uncle . William had enlisted in the Fifty-seventh Illinois Infantry on December 26, 1861, and was discharged on a surgeon's certificate of disability at Corinth, Mississippi, on June 24, 1862. William's younger brother James volunteered for Company D of the Thirty-fourth Illinois Infantry on January 29, 1864. This was a veteran regiment and the majority of the men were from Bureau and neighboring Lee County, although the name of twenty-two-year-old James M. Deaver, of Portsmouth, Scioto County, Ohio, also appears on the roster. He had enlisted in Company D of the Fifty-seventh Illinois on September 7, 1861.

Clearly William was initially somewhat at a loss for words, but he warmed to the task as he wrote.

Greenville, Illinois
April 27th 1864

Although not being much of a hand at letter writing or conveying my thoughts I thought that I would attempt to address you in this the silent way in which friends convey thoughts and wishes to friends at a distance. Therefore, wishing to hear from you and thinking that you may have a few spare moments and thoughts and would like to hear from this part of the world, I thought I would improve the time and visit for when I was in Dixie I greatly felt the influence of notes from home and friends and dreary passed the days when mail arrived and none for me. But this I suppose is not interesting and to tell the truth, I am at a loss to know what to write to you that will interest and entertain you for if you remember, I was young when you left here, but however, I will write what I think will interest you and if I fail you will please pardon.

This has been a cold, wet spring here so far. Farmers have not planted any corn as yet and the ground is too wet. Labor is high and hands are scarce. Farmers are paying from $20.00 to $28.00 per month. I will give you a partial price list of some things in market.

| | |
|---|---|
| Wheat from | $1.00–$1.29 per bushel |
| Corn from | .80–.90 per bushel |
| Oats | .60 –.70 per bushel |
| Potatoes | .75–.80 per bushel |
| Tea | 1.60 –2.20 per pound |
| Coffee | .40–.50 per pound |
| Calico from | .20–.28 per yard |
| Sheeting | .30–.55 per yard |

We have had a prospect of a Rail Road and there is talk that we will get it in two years, but it is almost too good news to be true.

Your time and part in this rebellion will soon be played out and I suppose you will not be sorry for hard and rough is the path of a soldier for dangerous missles fly therein. What do you think the end will be like and when will the end be. My opinion is the end is not yet neither will it be soon although I hope it will soon come to a close for many valuable lives have been lost in defense of the good old flag. But I fear many more will be lost. I have a brother in the 34th Ill. Vol. Co. D, at Camp Rossville, 8 miles from Chattanooga and I suppose he would be glad to see you if you make yourself known. You will find a number of boys from Walnut in that Company.

This place called Walnut has somewhat improved since you was here. We have a post office and two stores, two blacksmiths shops, two shoe shops and a ballroom besides doctors and drugs enough to physic the state.

Well Mc you remember that old fiddle you used to play and there was nothing remarkable about it, but I have learned to play a few tunes on it and many a time has it squealed a jig since you left Walnut and vicinity. But I guess I have written enough for this time. At least you will find it enough to puzzle your brain some time to read it. Therefore, I will close by asking you to write soon and as often as you can.

Your Nephew
William Landers

Adaline included her own brief comments at the end of the letter.

Dear Uncle,

I will try and write a few lines to you this morning, but I can only write a few line this time for I have not time for I have a chance to send to the P.O. if I hurry. I believe the folks are all as well as usual. I believe my husband is getting better slowly. I saw your photograph yesterday, the one that Aunt Euretta has. I thought it looked very natural. Mother has not got hers yet, but she is going after it as soon as she can. I must close this time as I shall not have a chance to send my letter. I will [write] a good long letter next time for I do not call this a letter, but I will try and do [better] after this. Write as soon as you can and when you write tell me how Aunt Mary and little Ella gets along.

From your affectionate Niece
Adaline E. Landers.

## *With General Sherman*

In 1864 Ohio native William Tecumseh Sherman succeeded Gen. Ulysses S. Grant as commander of the Military Division of the Mississippi for the western theater. During his campaign through northern Georgia, Sherman moved south toward Atlanta with three armies: the Army of the Cumberland under Maj. Gen. George H. Thomas, the Army of Tennessee under Maj. Gen. James B. McPherson, and the Army of the Ohio under Maj. Gen. John M. Schofield. The Thirty-third Ohio were, as part of the Army of the Cumberland, under Thomas. During this campaign they would face Confederate troops under Gen. Joseph E. Johnston who had replaced Braxton Bragg after his unsatisfactory performance at Chickamauga, his unsuccessful attempt to starve Union forces at Chattanooga, and later defeat at Dalton, Georgia.

The first major test the regiment would face in Sherman's Atlanta campaign was at Resaca, Georgia, from May 13 to 16. There, Confederate forces were entrenched upon a ridge just north of the small town of Resaca. On the second day of fighting, Sherman had ordered an attack upon the center of Johnston's forces by General Palmer's Fourteenth Corps. Men from the Thirty-third were unanimous in their views that only the brigade of Brig. Gen. William P. Carlin, was actually engaged in the ordered assault. The Thirty-third, part of Carlin's brigade, lost sixteen men killed and forty-two wounded. Four of the wounded would die later of wounds received that day. One of those wounded was Mary Ann's brother, Pvt. James Montgomery.

## *Battle of Resaca, Georgia*

22nd May 1864, Kingston, Georgia.
Dear wife. I have just a half a sheet of paper and I will make the most of it to give you a partial sketch of our movements since I wrote last. I wrote to you about the 2nd or 3rd of this month and for the want of paper I have not been able to write since. We left Ringgold on the 7th and began to skirmish with the enemy the same day and there has been more or less fighting every day since until the 19th.

On the 13th, 14th or 15th there was some hard fighting. Our reg't as usual had its share of losses. James was slightly wounded, but it is by no means serious. I was not in the fight. I was too lame to keep up with the company. I am not able to stand marching.

We are now within 54 miles from Atlanta & 75 from Chattanooga. Tomorrow the regt. marches with 20 days rations. Report says we are going to Cumberland gap, but there is no certainty. George is in camp about six miles from here. So is brother Newton [Company I, 31st Illinois Infantry]. I saw Jonathan Rockwell [Company A, 39th Ohio Infantry] today. He said George was well. I would have gone down and seen him today if I had been able. In this I send you two letters from Abigail. I also got one from Adaline's husband. When I write again, I will send it. Give my love to mother. Kiss Ella for me and believe me ever true. Your devoted husband.
Mc Montgomery
Mary Montgomery
Direct your next to Graysville, Ga.

As it would turn out, the wound suffered by James Montgomery was far more serious than originally believed. The gunshot wound in his right hand would, like many such wounds, develop gangrene. Fortunately for James, he did not lose his hand, but did carry for the remainder of his life, a useless hand with a large gaping hole in the center.

June 3, 1864 Near Dallas, Ga.

Dear wife. This is the first chance I have had to write for some time. We are here in front of the enemy and a continual skirmish kept up. Our reg't was on the front line for five days and was only relieved from the skirmish line yesterday evening. Yesterday afternoon I fired 30 shots at the rebs, but I could not count the number the rebs fired at me, but thanks to kind providence as yet I am unscathed. The rebels hold a very strong position here and the only apparent chance of dislodging them is to flank them out but every thing looks favorable and I think this company will soon have a successful termination and then I have no idea that I will ever have to pass through another. In my last I told you that James was slightly wounded at the battle of Snake Creek Gap. He was struck on the wrist, the left one, I think. There was no bone broken and if no accident occurs it will soon be well. I have not been very well since I came out this time. I have been lame and when we march I cannot keep up, but have to get along the best I can. But the time for my soldiering begins to look short and hope how soon it may end. George is here in this department some place, but I have never had a chance to see him, but it is raining and I have no shelter but a tree so I will have to quit. I want you to write to me soon. Send me a sheet of paper, envelope & stamp for this is my last. In directing to me be careful to put the regt. Brigade & Division. It makes but little difference for the rest. Still you may direct to Kingston, Ga. Give my love to mother. Kiss Ella for me and take good care of yourself and do not fret about me, for without God's will I cannot fall. Farewell, God bless you. From your affectionate husband,

Mc Montgomery

Mary Montgomery

The regiment would face continued contact with Johnston's forces, first at Cassville, Georgia, from May 19 to 22, and by Thursday, June 9, they had advanced to Kennesaw Mountain where the

Confederate forces were entrenched. The Thirty-third, under Major General Thomas, formed the center of Sherman's line with Schofield on the right and McPherson on the left. The fight to gain access to the town of Marietta, Georgia, which sat on the opposite side of the mountain, was crucial to Sherman's plan to control the Western and Atlantic Railroad, the supply line to Atlanta. First, however, they had to gain control of the mountain which was protected by Confederate artillery. The struggle dragged on through the month of June. Finally, Sherman abandoned his plan for a frontal assault and instead attempted to flank Johnston's army. This he successfully did and by July 2, Confederate forces abandoned their position.

> On the field June 5th [1864]
>
> Dear wife. I have an opportunity of writing a few lines this afternoon and I have been fortunate enough to get a half sheet of paper. Where I will [find] an envelope, I can't tell yet. John Weber [Webber, Company E, 33rd O.V.I.] wrote this morning. In his letter he stated that we was still confronting the enemy. Since then we have learned that they have left but I expect we will follow after them. I have not heard from James for several days. The last I heard from him he was doing well. The weather for the last day or two has been wet and rainy but we have fared very well. We come off of the skirmish line the day it began to rain and have not been back since.
>
> Last evening I was up to the 34 Ills regt. To see my old neighbors. They was all well except James Robinson (Newton's stepson). He lost an arm at the battle of Resaca. I am getting better of my lameness, but if we have much marching to do, I will have to stay behind. But you see my half sheet is about full so I must close. Give my love to mother. Tell Ella Pa has some hopes of coming home before long. Treasure up my heart's warmest love for yourself and write soon.
> Mc M. to Mary M.

It would be a little more than a month before Mary Ann would receive another letter from her husband.

## *Private Newton Montgomery's Plight*

Although the Montgomery family was unaware of the event, tragedy struck Pvt. Newton Montgomery on June 14, 1864, at Clifton, Tennessee. At nine o'clock on the evening of Monday, June 13, the Thirty-first Illinois Infantry had been ordered to march toward Mussel Shoals, Alabama, in pursuit of Confederate general Nathan Bedford Forrest. After marching all night, they learned that Forrest had escaped and they were ordered back to camp at Clifton. They arrived in camp at eleven o'clock in the morning, exhausted and hungry.

At two o'clock that afternoon the regiment went on dress parade on the sands of the river. It was an oppressively hot, cloudless day, and several soldiers were overcome by sunstroke. Pvt. Newton Montgomery had collapsed, unconscious on the parade ground and was carried to his tent where he remained unconscious until the next day. Newton's life was changed forever. He awoke to find that his right arm and leg were paralyzed. He had difficulty speaking and Amos N. Patten and James Crawford of the Thirty-first concluded that he was "partially insane." Newton was transported by boat to Ward 4, of the hospital at Mound City, Illinois. He was discharged on a surgeon's certificate of disability on December 19, 1864, at Quincy, Illinois.

Eighteen sixty-four would prove to have serious challenges to other soldiers of the Montgomery family, as well as to their friends in the service. Pvt. Samuel Roxby provided news regarding James as well as an update on his own condition. At the time, the usual "prescription" for medication to treat hospitalized soldiers for pain was one tablespoon of whisky twice a day. Needless to say, this provided minimal, if any, relief for their suffering.

July 16th -64 Browns Hospital, Louisville, Ky.
Friend Mc.
I have set down to write to you. I do not know if I shall be able or not. I have been very sick since I left you. I am just able to walk to the sink and back. I have taken a very heavy cold and the cough is killing me. I spit up green flem [sic] all the time. I think I am getting some better. I have a hard time getting here. I thought I should never get here alive. James is here. He has got a very [bad]

hand. The gangrene got in to it. It has left a hole in the back of his hand the size of a teacup. He will lose the use of his hand. The doctors was going to cut his arm off but they got the gangrene stopped. He is out of danger now. He never had any care taken of it until he got here. James has wrote home one time since he has been here. If there is any chance to get my (Prescription?) wrote, I should like to have it the chance he gets. I must stop now. Getting weak to hold the pen.

Direct your letter to Brown Hospital No. 7 Ward No. 6.
When you write to James direct to Ward 12 Tent 6.
Write as soon as you get this.
Samuel Roxby

When Mary Ann finally received another letter from McLain, she was relieved to learn that he was in good health. It was also comforting to learn that despite the brutality of war, there were times when soldiers from both sides of the struggle, welcomed the opportunity for any cessation of violence and the chance to share a cup of coffee with a fellow soldier.

July 18, 1864
In the field four miles west of Atlanta Ga.

Dearest wife. I have just finished your letter written on the third and I cannot express my gratitude to you for the welcome message. The only way I can repay you at the present is to send you this by return mail. I am in good health at present and if I could keep from thinking of home so much, I would be as well content as I have been since I came in the service. But the nearer my time is out the more impatient I get, but I hope the end of my service is close at hand.

Now I expect you would like to know how we spend our time down her in Dixie. Well, I will tell you we have a deep ditch that we live in. It is situated very near the rebels. So near that neither them or us dare show our head above the ground. Today, however, it is different. We are not fighting much. In fact the boys was on very friendly terms for a while this morning visiting each other and trading coffee and tobacco. I went over and traded coffee for tobacco and stayed with them for nearly an hour. After I came back the rebels had orders to commence firing, but before they would fire, they hollered, "Yanks get in your holes, we are going to shoot." But they are not daring today whether they kill a yank or not so we do not keep near so close today as usual. But we do not know when the calm may be broken or where the bolt will strike when the storm bursts. Our line is several miles long and at no point is our lines father from the enemy than from mother's to John Ke[n]nedy's. Where we are it is not more than half that far. The weather is very hot down here and a great portion of [the] time we have to lay in the ditch where no air can get to us and the sun coming down makes it disagreeable enough but I am willing to bear almost anything to crush this accursed rebellion. My three years work in the field is almost done, but my work for the Union will never be done until an honorable peace is restored and woe to the Northern traitor that crosses my path after I get home. I have more respect today for the rebels here in our front that are shooting at us all the time than I have for them. But the mail will go on in fifteen minutes so I must make the most of my time. Jonathan Snyder [Company C, 39th O.V.I.] was over to see me a few days ago. He said George was well. I would go over and see him but I can't leave very well for we can never tell when we will have to move. He is about two miles from here and if nothing happens, I will see him before I start home. If you get this within a few days you had better answer it and send me more paper. I don't get a bit of paper only as you send it. That is the reason you don't hear from me oftener. But don't be uneasy. If you don't hear from me again until I get home though, if I can get paper and envelopes I will write again. Answer this any how and if I should be gone when the answer comes it will be sent back. Take care of yourself and Ella. Trust in God who has been my protector so far and I trust he will spare me to get back to you and Ella. Give my love to mother and pray for your absent husband.

Mc Montgomery

Mary Montgomery

P.S. Tell Osborn that I saw Arthur a few days ago. He was well. Sid Brown [corporal, Company A], John Weber [corporal, Company E] and Luis Porshot [private, Company E, 33rd] is well. Mc

**CHAPTER 14**

# The Siege of Atlanta

---

## Battle of Peachtree Creek

On July 18, Maj. Gen. William Sherman sent instructions to Maj. Gen. George Thomas regarding a plan to launch a push toward Atlanta. Sherman would take the main road while Thomas was to swing left across the south fork of Peachtree Creek. From there he was to join the forces of Maj. Gen. John McAllister Schofield from the north with Maj. Gen. James Birdseye McPherson approaching from the east. It was Sherman's hope that Confederate Joseph Johnston might give up Atlanta without a fight. Apparently, the Confederate government at Richmond feared that Johnston might just do that. On Sunday night, July 17, Johnston received word from Samuel Cooper, adjutant and inspector general of the Confederate army that he was relieved of his command of the Army and Department of Tennessee. The communiqué informed him that Lt. Gen. John B. Hood would immediately replace him. The battle continued for the next several days, but by Friday, July 22, the Union army had advanced to within two miles of Atlanta.

Atlanta Ga July 26th 1864

My Dear wife; I received your welcome letter several days ago, but circumstances over which I had no control have prevented me from answering it. Since I wrote to you before, we have had hard work and plenty of it. On the 18th, the day I received your letter, we crossed the Chattahoochie River and advanced two miles. I should have remarked however that on the fifth we advanced 6 miles and had a sharp skirmish with the enemy at the river afore-mentioned. Our loss in the reg't on the fifth was 17 men killed & wounded. Four out of that number belonged to Co. A. We then rested until the 18th On the 19th we again moved forward. The rebels disputing every foot of ground. That day we gained about 2 miles. On the 20th we crossed Peach Tree Creek and fortified in the evening. The rebels charged our lines but was driven back with severe loss. There was two wounded in Co. A. that day. On the 21st we moved forward again. Co. A. on the skirmish line. In less than half mile we encountered the enemy. The fight was stubborn. The combatants not more than 40 paces apart. Co. A's loss was one killed and four wounded. We held the ground however and the next morning we advanced to our present position meeting with but little resistance. We are not yet in possession of the town but we are in plain view of it and our big guns can easily reach it. We are well fortified and with nothing more than the present force in front of us we can hold our position. At the present there is but little fighting going on. The rebels is shelling us a little but we do not mind that much. The weather has been very warm down here and it still continues.

So now, Dearest, Mary, about my coming home. I was in hopes that I would be able [to] start home by the fifth of next month, but I fear I will be disappointed I expect I will have to stay until the 27th any how and perhaps longer. But be assured, Dear Mary, I will not be absent a day longer than I can help. On the 20th, I rec'd a letter from Mr. Roxby. He is at the same hospital with James. He writes that James has a very sore hand but it was getting better. I have not heard from Ill. for a long time. I have not written for the want of paper and envelopes. I write to no one now but you and I hope to depend on you for the material to do even that. But I trust the time is not far distant when I will have no occasion to write to you. You must keep up our courage and trust in God. He alone can guard and protect us. He has been merciful to me more than I deserve. Yet, I hope he will yet spare me to return to you and my darling child.

Pray for me dear Mary and if it should be the will of Heaven that [we] meet no more here on earth, remember the cause I battle for is just and look forward to a home where wars never separate and trouble never comes. But do not let what I have written give you a single despondent thought because the dangers to come cannot be greater than those already past and for your sake I will do nothing rash. Give my love to mother. Kiss Ella for her pa and Mary God Bless you.
Mc Montgomery
Mary Montgomery

P.S. Send one more sheet of paper, stamp and envelope. Direct to Marietta, Ga.

## A Strange Foreboding

As Mary read the final paragraph of his letter, she gasped at a sudden tightening in her chest. It felt as though a sharp blow had suddenly made it impossible to breathe. Again, she felt that strange foreboding fear that seemed to hover over her. She and little Ella had endured so many long nights without her husband and now the fear arose in her throat again with the possibility that the new life she carried inside her might also be denied a father's love.

On Sunday, August 14, 1864, Sergeant Montgomery was wounded during fighting in and around Atlanta, Georgia. He had, of course, been wounded in battle before, and the initial evaluation of the doctors was that although severe, the wound was not dangerous. However, Lt. George Winkler wrote to Mary to inform her of her husband's injury. He also assured her that her husband would no doubt be sent home within a few weeks.

Battlefield near Atlanta, Ga.
Aug. 16th, 1864
Mrs. Montgomery, in compliance with a request made by your husband, I take this first opportunity to inform you that on the 14th of Aug, he received a severe wound in the left arm just above

the elbow. I am truly glad that his wound is no worse than it is and would just say to you that you need not be alarmed in the least in regard to his welfare, for I do assure you that his wound is not a dangerous one. He has been sent back to the Hospital. I think that you may look for him home in two or three weeks. Louis Pours-chot (Co. E) received a severe wound the same day. I must close for the present. Please give my love to all my folks and tell them to write to me. I remain yours with respect.
George C Winkler, Lieut.
Commanding Co A. 33rd O.V.I.

A day later, Sergeant Montgomery wrote to Mary to reassure her that he was doing well, but that it had been necessary to amputate his arm. He promised to write again soon.

Hospital near Marietta. Aug. 17th '64
I can only scribble a line or two. Was wounded last Sunday. The ball passed through my arm just above the elbow. To save my arm was out of the question. The wound is doing well. Do not be uneasy. I will get north before long. I will write again in a day or two. Give my love to mother. Don't get down hearted. Kiss Ella for her pa. I can't tell you how to direct at the present for there is no telling when we leave.
Ever yours
Mc Montgomery
Mary Montgomery

Mary was not the only family member to be concerned about the welfare of Sergeant Montgomery. Word of Gen. William Tecumseh Sherman's southern surge through Georgia was a topic of discussion throughout the country and family from Illinois were concerned that they had received no news from their brother in months.

September 2, 1864
Greenville, Bureau Co. Ill.

Dear Sister and Brother

It has been a long time since I have heard from you. We thought it time to break the silence. We have all written to the army to differ-ent places but have not had a word from McLain since in the Spring when he sent us his photographs and as we are aware that his time is out unless he has reenlisted, we think strange of his not writing to any of us and in fact we are worried, so we can rest no longer and will now write to Wheelersburg and see if we can not learn something of the cause. I am now at Mr. Janes house. We are generally quite well though some of us are still complaining. Wm. Landers health is very poor. His disease is of the lungs. Mr. Janes health is [the] same, better than it used to be but not the best yet. The rest of us have nothing to complain [about].

The lower portion of the first page of this letter is missing as is a part of page two and some passages are not legible.

I do not know what you—we all feel so anxious about . . .

Mr. Janes is making molasses again this fall and he says if you are a coming west he thinks it time you was about it. They have a big fat baby two months old. She says to tell McLain to come and name him. I do not know of anything interesting. I guess I will have to close by asking you to write us a long letter and tell us about McLain. If he is not at home we all send our love to you and want you should write as soon as you get this.

From you sister and friend
Yours Truly
Abigail A. Montgomery

## The Dreaded News Arrives

Late in the evening on September 4, Mary began a letter to her husband, but was consumed with worry and as her daughter wanted to know why she was crying, she put down the letter to finish later.

Wheelersburg, Sept. 4th 1864
Dear Husband.
I take the present opportunity to answer your letters. One dated 23, 25. I was very glad to hear form you. You did not tell me whether you have had your arm taken off. The folks say that you have had it taken off. I hope that it is not so. I was in hopes that you would not get wounded any more I am sorry that you have to suffer so much. I want you to take good care of yourself. [torn page]

I hope that you will get well soon. I am tolerable well. I am troubled so about you that I don't know what to do some times. I want you to write as often as you can. We heard from George the 14 of Aug. He was well then. We have not heard from James since the 17th of July. Ella is well and all the rest of the folks is well. I will send you four stamps this time although I had to pay only three cents. That's as cheap as to send you stamps. I had a letter from Lieutenant George B. Winkler and three from you. I sent one to [not legible]

Before Mary Ann could finish this letter, the terrible news reached her that her husband had died.

# CHAPTER 15

# War's Deadly Toll

The country experienced a devastating loss of life during the Civil War. Current estimates indicate that more than six hundred thousand American soldiers died while serving in the Union and Confederate armies. The staggering reality is that more American men lost their lives in this war than the total lives lost in all other wars in which this country has been involved since the American Revolution.

In terms of the comparative importance of the contributions of Ohio and Illinois to the war effort, Ohio provided more men per capita than any other state. The total number of Ohio troops was exceeded only by New York and Pennsylvania, and Ohio suffered the second highest number of deaths after New York. Illinois was fourth in the number of men serving and in the number of deaths. Aside from the number who died during the war, many thousands more were permanently disabled and thus the economic welfare of themselves and their families was forever altered. Certainly the Montgomery families of Ohio and Illinois were among those who suffered greatly. Their experiences during and after the war would have been common to most families in these Midwestern states.

## *Thaddeus Delorain Montgomery 1826–94*

McLain Montgomery's brother Thaddeus "Dell" Montgomery was discharged from Company B, Sixty-fourth Illinois Volunteer Infantry, on a surgeon's certificate of disability on March 4, 1863. In 1876, Del Montgomery sought medical treatment from Dr. A. H. Thompson of Princeton, Illinois. Dr. Thompson determined that Del suffered from a cancerous condition of the ribs on the left side of the chest. Dr. William M. Kaull, of Bureau County examined Del on July 21, 1880, upon his request for an increase in his pension. Dr. Kaull's report detailed the causes of his failing eyesight as "congestion of the retina; vessels tortuous and much enlarged." His report further described the complications that had resulted from the wound Del had received at Corinth, and which had produced a tumor at the sight of the wound. The tumor had remained untreated for several years and was finally removed by Dr. Kaull, only to have the tumors reappear. The doctor estimated that Del Montgomery should be entitled to a pension of six dollars per month. In 1883 Del received an increase in his pension bringing it to twelve dollars per month. Thaddeus Delorain Montgomery died May 14,1894, in Greenville, Illinois, of heart disease and dropsy. He was sixty-eight years old. His widow, Abigail, died September 27, 1910, of cancer.

## *Isaac Newton Montgomery 1830–1910*

McLain Montgomery's brother Newton had enlisted in Company I, Thirty-first Regiment Illinois Infantry, on December 30, 1863, at age thirty-three, and was discharged under a surgeon's certificate of disability on December 19, 1864, after suffering a stroke. Newton's wife had been upset that her husband was in the army and blamed him for her son's enlistment. When her son, James H. Robinson, was wounded on May 14, 1864, at the battle of Resaca, Georgia, and lost his arm as a result, she decided she had had enough. After her son's discharge, she brought him home and tended to his care. She also filed for divorce from her husband, Newton.

Although Newton's condition had improved slightly over time, he never regained full use of his arm or leg. On December 19, 1864, he applied for a pension based upon the disability he had suffered in the army, and received fifteen dollars per month. It appears that after his return to Illinois he drifted through life, eventually leaving his family in Bureau County and, thereafter, was forced to rely on assistance from others.

In addition to the disabling stroke he suffered while in the army and the divorce from his wife of six years, Newton appears to have been a lost soul moving from place to place. No record has been found of his whereabouts until 1890 when he was enumerated on the Veteran's Schedule for Cedar County, Nebraska. Clearly, Newton's mental capacities had diminished and although he correctly identified his company and regiment, he claimed to have been a captain of his company and reported that he had been wounded five times and was thus, unable to work. On March 25, 1896, he was living in Lyons, Nebraska, and applied for an increase in pension. He was examined by a physician who described his condition and noted that he weighed only 115 pounds. The doctor also noted that Newton had, at some time in his life, been shot just above the right elbow. Newton gave March 3, 1887, as the date of the accident. By the following year, 1897, he was unable to remember either the names or dates of birth of his three daughters.

Newton died of kidney and heart trouble on June 28, 1910, at the home of his neighbor Thomas Tierney of Lyons, Nebraska, who had been caring for him for the previous five months. Thomas Tierney submitted to the commission of pensions a request for funds to cover the costs of burial, which totaled $69.15. On September 16, 1910, sixty-eight-year-old John D. McKinnie of Burt County, Nebraska, applied to the commissioner of pensions for reimbursement from the pension of Isaac Newton Montgomery for expenses for his care. It was reported that at the time of his death Newton's net worth was thirty dollars.

## George W. Montgomery 1835–65

Mary Ann's brother George Montgomery, a private in the Thirty-ninth Ohio Volunteer Infantry, died May 31, 1865, in Washington, D.C., of typhoid fever contracted while in the service. His widow, Mary C. Modes Montgomery, had during her youth, moved many times with her parents, Christian and Elizabeth Modes, and her nine siblings. Her parents were both emigrants from Germany who had arrived in Baltimore, Maryland, by 1837. Christian, a weaver by trade, remained in Maryland until 1841 when he moved his family to Virginia and remained there until 1847. They next located in Allegheny, Pennsylvania, until 1856 when they moved to southern Ohio, settling first in Portsmouth and finally in Wheelersburg, Porter Township. Upon the death of her husband, George, Mary applied for a pension and received eight dollars per month. She returned to the home of her parents, who were living in Beaver Falls, Pennsylvania, in 1870. By 1877 Mary had moved to LaSalle County, Illinois, where two of her siblings made an affidavit on her behalf in her attempt to retrieve pension payments that were in arrears. It appears that her propensity for moving around posed a problem for the government in its efforts to verify her identity and make payments promptly. Her last known residence was in the state of Missouri. While still in her early twenties, she had suffered the loss of her infant daughter and the death of her husband to the war, and lived the remainder of her life as a widow.

## James Montgomery 1842–1935

Mary Anne's brother, Pvt. James Montgomery of the Thirty-third Ohio, returned home from the war with a permanently disabled hand from the wound received at the battle of Resaca, Georgia. He was mustered out December 20, 1864, on the expiration of his term of service. He returned to his home in Wheelersburg and Mary Ann and her two daughters along with her mother, Nancy, lived in the same household with James who remained a bachelor throughout his life.

He applied for and received a pension in January of 1865. His mother, Nancy Montgomery, died January 3, 1900, at age ninety-two.

In 1903 Nelson W. Evans, a well-known local historian and author, published *A History of Scioto County, Ohio, together with a Pioneer Record of Southern Ohio.* Volume two contains, on pages 1076 and 1077, a biographical sketch of James Montgomery. An abbreviated portion of that sketch appears below.

> There is no citizen of Scioto County who is prouder of his army service, or has more reason to be. His heart is warm to every comrade of the Civil War. He is a man highly esteemed by his neighbors. Even the tongue of the gossiping busy-body can not find material here for evil speaking. He minds his own business strictly, religiously attends the services of his own church, looks after his farming interests and other business matters in a quiet, gentlemanly, unobtrusive way, and comes as near having absolutely no enemies as any man that can be found. Although he went to war, and carries a hand almost useless from the effects of Confederate bullets, yet he is a man of peace. He lives unmarried at his ancestral home on Dogwood Ridge, enjoying the products of his fertile lands, and surrounded on all sides by appreciative friends.

James Montgomery died of heart disease on June 6, 1925, in Portsmouth, Scioto County, Ohio.

## Ellis Montgomery 1830–62

Cousin Ellis Montgomery enlisted at age thirty-one in Company A, Thirty-ninth Ohio Infantry, on July 16, 1861. He was discharged on April 11, 1862, under a surgeon's certificate of disability and died seven months later on November 13, 1862, of consumption. Ellis had married Elizabeth Chapman on May 4, 1853, in Scioto County, and the couple had three children. On September 1, 1867, his widow, Elizabeth married Job Kittle, a native of Randolph County, Virginia. On March 22, 1877, Job died and Elizabeth was yet again a widow. In her attempts to get a widow's pension she encountered difficulties in providing proof that Ellis Montgomery's death was caused by health problems incurred while in the army.

Recordkeeping was far from adequate, and the regimental surgeon for the Thirty-ninth Ohio, Dr. Christian Foster, had died while on a trip to Europe in May 1887, just eight months before Elizabeth applied for a pension. A further complication was the fact that Dr. Dennison, who had been his family physician, was also deceased. The issue was finally settled to the government's satisfaction by an affidavit provided by John C. Musser who had been first lieutenant and later captain of Company A of the Thirty-ninth Ohio. Captain Musser stated that Pvt. Ellis Montgomery was an able-bodied man at the time of his enlistment, but after a hard campaign in the winter of 1861 and early 1862 in northern Missouri and in the campaign of New Madrid he had become quite ill. Captain Musser recalled that he was discharged at New Madrid, Missouri, in April 1862 for disability, and in his words: "He coughed a good deal about that time and spit up a very bad corruption, until some of the men in his mess complained about it." He noted that he had learned that Ellis had died from lung disease shortly after his return home. The widow Kittle was granted a pension of twelve dollars a month. She died September 4, 1909, in Scioto County, Ohio.

## Homer Montgomery 1838–1924

Homer Montgomery, brother of Ellis, enlisted as a corporal on July 16, 1861, at age twenty in Company A, Thirty-ninth Infantry, and was promoted to commissary sergeant and finally to first lieutenant on January 11, 1865. He was mustered out on July 9, 1865, at Louisville, Kentucky. On October 14, 1865, Homer married Elizabeth Willey in Scioto County, where the couple lived and Homer worked as a carpenter for the next twenty years or so.

Homer applied for and received a pension on December 24, 1886, and the following year the family moved to Florida. Perhaps the move was prompted by their concerns over the health of their oldest son, Albert, who had tuberculosis. Albert never married, but resided with his parents until the spring of 1894 when he returned to Scioto County and the home of his grandfather where he died on Saturday,

May 27, 1894.

In 1900 sixty-one-year-old Homer and forty-eight-year-old Elizabeth, or "Lizzie," as she was known, were living in Paola, Orange County, Florida. Lizzie reported that she had given birth to three children who were all deceased. Lizzie died two years later near Sandford, Florida, on May 30, 1902. After the death of his wife, Homer returned to Scioto County where he died on Tuesday, June 28, 1904, at the home of his brother, William Henry Harrison Montgomery on Offnere Street in Portsmouth, Ohio.

## William H. H. Montgomery 1834—before 1930

A third son of Abraham Montgomery, William Henry Harrison Montgomery, was one of the many Ohio men who answered Governor Brough's request for men to serve for one hundred days service. Twenty-three-year-old William enlisted on August 2, 1864, in Company F of the 140th Ohio Volunteers and was mustered out on September 3, 1864, at Gallipolis, Ohio. After the war, William and his wife, the former Eugenie Herbert, lived in Portsmouth, Ohio, where William worked in a dry goods store. Eldest son, Arthur, clerked in a grocery store and son Earl was a conductor on a streetcar. His daughter Lucy and her husband Charles Warnock lived with William and Eugenie in 1910. Charles was employed as a cutter in a shoe factory.

## Charles Montgomery, alias Montgomery Honchell, 1841–65

Twenty-three-year-old Charles Montgomery had enlisted as a private in Company A of the Thirty-ninth Ohio on July 16, 1861, which happened to be the same day that both Ellis and Homer Montgomery enlisted. Charles was 5 feet 8 1/2 inches tall, with gray eyes, brown hair, and a dark complexion. He stated that he was born in Scioto County, Ohio, and was, at the time of his enlistment, a farmer in that county. One would suspect that he was at least related, if not a brother to Homer and Ellis Montgomery who enlisted in the same regiment on the same day. However, that assumption would be challenged upon the death of Pvt. Charles Montgomery.

Private Montgomery had re-enlisted in 1863 for an additional three years, but he died January 25, 1865, of chronic diarrhea in Cumberland General Hospital at Nashville, Tennessee. It should be noted that Charles, unlike the other Montgomery men of Scioto County, had not received any formal education and could neither read nor write. His enlistment papers bear his mark rather than his signature. The official record of death and interment recorded by the army states that he was married to Mrs. Martha Montgomery of Powellsville, Scioto County, Ohio, and official notification of the soldier's death was sent to her at that address.

The peculiarities arose when his widow applied for a pension. A number of unusual documents and affidavits were produced in support of her claim. On August 29, 1865, eighteen-year-old Martha Honchell, resident of Buffalo Furnace, Greenup County, Kentucky, appeared before Judge C. B. Egarton of the Probate Court of Lawrence County, Ohio, and swore that she was the widow of Montgomery Honchell, alias Charles Montgomery, a private in Company A of the Thirty-ninth Ohio Volunteer Infantry. She stated that she had married Montgomery Honchell on January 24, 1864, in Lawrence County, Ohio, and that her maiden name was Martha Birch. The pension bureau denied her application for a pension, pending clarification of the soldier's identity.

Between the time of Martha's initial application for a widow's pension in 1865 through the intervening years until 1869, several relatives, neighbors, and friends filed affidavits in support of her application. They testified that they had witnessed the marriage of the couple and that the soldier's true name was Montgomery Honchell. One of the witnesses was an elderly woman named Margaret Swyers who swore that she was the mother of the soldier in question. She stated that her son had written to her and others in 1865 that he had a furlough and wanted them to come after him and so she went to Cumberland Hospital in Nashville, Tennessee. Upon her arrival she was informed that her son was called Charles Montgomery on the army's records. Margaret claimed that she had no idea why her son had changed his name but suspected that he must have been intoxicated at the time. She further described how she had stayed with her son until he died and also swore that Martha Birch Honchell was her son's widow.

Next a document was produced, purportedly dictated by and signed by Charles Montgomery on January 23, 1865, just two days before his death at the Cumberland General Hospital in Nashville, Tennessee. Again, an "x" was marked as the soldier's signature. The statement read as follows:

> I Charles Montgomery a private of Co. A 39th Regt. Ohio Vol. Inf. Being sane and in my right mind do hereby of my own free will and choice give and bequeath to my mother, Margaret Swyers all my property, personal or real except what lawfully belong to my wife Martha Montgomery.

Late in 1869 Martha Honchell eventually received a pension based upon the service of Charles Montgomery in Company A of the Thirty-ninth Ohio. She also received the $340.00 in back pay that had been due Private Montgomery at the time of his death.

There is an 1860 census record for then thirteen-year-old Martha Birch, daughter of James W. and Melinda Birch. There is not, however, a census record in 1870 for either Martha Montgomery or Martha Honchell, nor is there a record for Margaret Swires/Swyers after the signing of her affidavit before justice of the peace in Scioto County on January 25, 1869. It seems likely that Margaret Swires was an unwed mother and the identity of the man who fathered the soldier known as Charles Montgomery, alias Montgomery Honchell, remains a mystery.

## McLain Armstrong Montgomery 1832–64

News of the death of Sgt. McLain Montgomery quickly spread throughout the community; however, it was some time before Mary Ann was able to learn details of her husband's final days. When Cyrus M. Finch, a physician from Wheelersburg, returned home from the war he provided information in support of Mary Ann's application for a widow's pension.

Cyrus Finch was serving in late August 1864, as surgeon of the Ninth Ohio Volunteer Cavalry. Upon learning of Sergeant Montgomery's injury, he visited him in the hospital at Chattanooga. He was saddened and shocked at what he saw.

> On or about the 29th day of August 1864, having learned that said McLain Montgomery was lying at Hospital in Chattanooga, Tennessee, I called to see him, and found him suffering with Hospital Gangrene of one [of] the arms, he having previous to this time received a gunshot wound in the same. The gangrene had at that time expanded upward and had involved the shoulder. He was delirious, and unable to recognize me. On inquiry of his attending physician he regarded him as being unable to live but a short time. My own opinion coincided with his physician. A few days afterwards I learned he had died. [Deposition given on January 26, 1867, in support of widow's application for a pension.]

There are discrepancies in the official records regarding the date of Sergeant Montgomery's death. His military service record lists his date of death as November 1, 1864; however, 1st Lt. Sylvester Keller who was in command of Company A, submitted in his report that Sergeant Montgomery died on September 5, 1864, and the official record of death and interment give September 5, as the date for both events. Based on the statement given by Dr. Finch regarding the critical nature of his condition on August 29, it appears that September 5 is the most likely date of death. McLain Armstrong Montgomery was thirty-one years old at the time of his death. He is buried in the National Cemetery at Chattanooga, Tennessee.

# *Epilogue*

*Where the treasure is, there will the heart be also.*
*Sergeant McLain Montgomery*
*To his wife, Mary Ann*
*from Greysville, Georgia, April 7, 1864*

Mary Ann's world seemed to collapse around her when she learned of her husband's death. Her worst fears were now a reality. She found it hard to shake off the deep depression that consumed her, and she feared for the well-being of the child she was carrying. It was with a great sense of relief that she was delivered of a second child on November 13, 1864. The child, a daughter, was named Anna McLain Montgomery.

Mary Ann dedicated her-

*Anna McLain Montgomery*
*The daughter he never knew.*

self to the education of her daughters and took delight in the interest the two showed in music and in the books that she had shared with her husband. Ella and Anna grew to womanhood, married, and had children of their own, but for them as for their mother, their lives had been forever altered by the death of McLain Montgomery. Daughter Ella remained in Scioto County, Ohio, throughout her life. She married in 1882 and she and her husband, John G. Fritz, had ten children and numerous grandchildren. One of those grandchildren was little Imogene Kinley, who loved to sit in the old rocker with her grandmother on the porch of the farmhouse on Dogwood Ridge.

*Four generations of Montgomery women.*
*Seated from left, Mary Ann Montgomery and Imogene Kinley.*
*Standing from left, Ella Montgomery Fritz and Mabel Fritz Kinley.*

For the next sixty-six years of her life, Mary Ann clung to the memory of her husband and held dear the letters that she treasured. Upon her death in 1930, her daughter Anna became the caretaker of the letters. Anna McLain Montgomery married her cousin, Byron A. Janes, son of Albina Montgomery and Alexander Hamilton Janes, on December 14, 1893, in Bureau County, Illinois, and later moved back to Scioto County, Ohio. Anna, like her mother, cherished the bequest until her own death in October of 1960 when the precious documents along with the photos, hand-carved crutch and journal were passed to Mary Ann's great-granddaughter, Eloise. Through her efforts, these treasured memories have been preserved as an important reminder of a Civil War family's proud heritage of service and sacrifice.

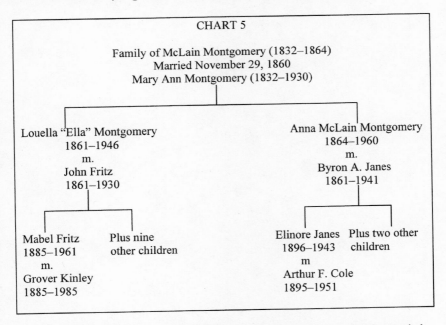

CHART 5

Family of McLain Montgomery (1832–1864)
Married November 29, 1860
Mary Ann Montgomery (1832–1930)

Louella "Ella" Montgomery
1861–1946
m.
John Fritz
1861–1930

Mabel Fritz
1885–1961
m.
Grover Kinley
1885–1985

Plus nine
other children

Anna McLain Montgomery
1864–1960
m.
Byron A. Janes
1861–1941

Elinore Janes
1896–1943
m
Arthur F. Cole
1895–1951

Plus two other
children

McLain Montgomery and Mary Ann Montgomery were first cousins. Mabel Fritz, granddaughter of the couple, and her husband, Grover Kinley, had three children, none of whom are shown on the chart. The oldest of their children was Imogene, or "Jeanne" who died May 19, 2010.

Anna McLain Montgomery married her first cousin, Byron A. Janes, son of Albina Montgomery and Alexander H. Janes. Their daughter, Elinor Janes, married Arthur Cole. They had three children, the youngest of whom is Eloise Cole Egbert. Imogene and Eloise, two of the great-granddaughters of McLain and Mary Ann, shared their personal remembrances of a Civil War widow with the author.

# Author's Notes
# and
# Acknowledgments

The letters, which were the inspiration and primary source for this book, are those written by McLain Montgomery beginning in 1853. The earliest of these were written from Bureau County, Illinois, where McLain, his mother and siblings had moved after the death of his father, John B. Montgomery, in Ohio in 1839. These early letters provide a glimpse into ways in which life was different for those on the prairie of northern Illinois than for those who remained behind in the hills of southern Ohio. Yet, through the years, especially during the tragic and bloody conflict of the Civil War, the shared experiences of this extended family is a microcosm of the experiences common to so many families who endured this national crisis.

As noted, the letters in this collection begin in 1853, while the story of the Montgomery family begins much earlier with their arrival in Southern Ohio in 1798. The family was large with a number of men who would eventually serve in the Union army and a number of mothers, wives and children who would be left at home to maintain the family farm and to worry for the safety of their loved ones.

The members of this family were a close-knit group of well-educated individuals who no doubt corresponded among themselves on a regular basis. But, unfortunately, those early letters are no longer in existence. The problem lay in how best to tell the story of this family, and introduce the reader to its many members in a consistent format and style that would be interesting, informative and true to historic facts. I decided to provide the details during those early years as though the information had been shared through letters, and other contemporary accounts. These are creative in presentation, but nonetheless, are based upon extensive research. The viewpoint from which the story unfolds fluctuates among those who would have had first hand knowledge to relate to other family members. The time period from 1853 through 1864 relies heavily upon the experiences and life of Sergeant McLain Montgomery and of his cousin and wife, Mary Ann Montgomery. It was Mary Ann, the Civil War widow, who became the caretaker of the letters.

In the collection, are several pieces of correspondence from family members in Bureau County, Illinois, as well as from neighbors in southern Ohio. But the majority of the letters are those written to Mary Ann by her husband, Sgt. McLain Montgomery. However, those few exceptions from his family in Illinois, also offer a private look at their shared wartime experiences from 1861 until Sergeant Montgomery's death in 1864. These letters chronicle the life of one family caught in the crisis of the Civil War. Their story would have been similar to those of thousands of other families who felt the impact of a war, and from which none would survive unscathed.

As important as these letters are, they also present certain challenges for the researcher. Letters written at the time of an important historic event, offer wonderful insight regarding what was significant to the writer and likewise to the recipient. But we cannot know with certainty what comments or questions have provoked a particular response. We can envision, for instance, that a wife and young mother, suddenly left to her own devices just a few days after giving birth to her first child, would certainly have been saddened and overwhelmed by a myriad of responsibilities for which she had neither prior training nor experience. Coupled with this she surely would have been frightened and concerned for her soldier husband's welfare. In such situations, I have supplied the reader with a description of how Mary Ann Montgomery might have felt upon reading her husband's letters. Hopefully, I have not attributed false behaviors or unfair characteristics to any of those whose lives I have described.

The first draft of the manuscript was complete by the spring of 2009. At that time, I asked friends and family to read it and offer critiques and suggestions. Their comments were very helpful, and revealed several issues that required editing. That process resulted in many false starts and stops, as well as a fair amount of frustration.

Perhaps the most daunting challenge lay in the scope of the information provided. The story covers the lives of four generations of the Montgomery family and more than thirty individual members. From the beginning, I had stubbornly insisted that this would not be a genealogy of one particular family, but rather would provide a broad picture of the experiences that would have been common to many families. But the truth of the matter was that the introduction of so many members of this family without some sort of relationship chart resulted in confusion for the reader. In an attempt to clarify the relationships, abbreviated genealogy charts were added.

The charts themselves also were a problem since the question of the paternity of Charles Montgomery, alias Montgomery Honchell, remained a mystery. Despite the appearance of Margaret Swyers who claimed to be the soldier's mother and swore that she had been by her son's deathbed at Cumberland Hospital in Nashville, Tennessee, in 1865, no official documentation to confirm her claim has been found. The decision to include available information regarding the soldier's military record was based upon the fact that several genealogical records prepared by Montgomery family members over the years included Charles Montgomery as a child of William Montgomery, Jr. It should be noted, however, that none of the letters written by family members over the years ever mention this man.

Another dilemma emerged during the multiple rewrites. The new issue was how best to assure the reader that the material presented was based upon fact and solid research without being cumbersome. I originally had provided endnotes, which require the reader to first refer to the back of the book for the source and from there to the bibliographic entry for specifics. Personally, I find this method to be not only burdensome, but also annoying.

Next I reverted to my preferred method, i.e., parenthetical notation within the body of the text. That eliminates at least one step in the reader's search for the source material. The problem with this method was that it interrupted the flow of the narrative.

Another difficulty resulted from the extensive amount of documents that had been collected and preserved by descendants of McLain and Mary Ann Montgomery after the widow's death in 1930. In addition to the letters themselves and the Civil War journal kept by Sergeant Montgomery, the collection included land deeds, marriage and death certificates, obituaries of family members as well as a variety of newspaper clippings pertaining to the family. For details of the personal lives of family members I relied heavily upon information from their obituaries and contemporary news accounts. This was especially the case for details of the murder of young Salina Montgomery and for verification of the friendship of the Montgomery family with the famous Indian Chief Shabbona. These were important and informative sources, but they often lacked either the date or place of publication. After much deliberation and frustration over the issue, I decided to omit footnotes altogether, and rely solely upon the Bibliography.

Because of this decision, I feel obligated to provide the reader with some suggestions as to where they might locate, within the Bibliography, source information that might be helpful for selected cases.

The description in chapter two of the undesirable prairie climate was based primarily on the statements made by James Monroe to Thomas Jefferson after Monroe had visited the area. His description can be found on page 117 in *The Writings of James Monroe* edited by Stanislaus Murray Hamilton, 1898.

Details regarding the life of Chief Shabbona were gleaned from a variety of sources and some are available from the Bureau County Historical Society Museum Gift Shop in Princeton, Illinois. One of those sources was *Memories of Shaubena* by Nehemiah Matson, 1878. Another important source was *History of Kane County*, Illinois by R. Waite Joslyn and Frank W. Joslyn which includes a diary entry by Laura Allen Bowers titled "Some Things I remember of Chief Shabbona," 1908.

Much of the background research for chapter seven, "Women at Home and Those at the Front," is based upon information from several sources including *They Fought Like Demons* by De Anne Blanton and Lauren M. Cook, 2002; *Bonnet Brigades* by Mary Elizabeth Massey, 1966; *Women During the Civil War: An Encyclopedia*, by Judith E. Harper, 2004; and Catherine Clinton's *Public Women of the Confederacy*, 1999. I am also indebted to Elizabeth Ann Topping of Columbus, Ohio, who provided not only, the photographic images of prostitutes used in the book, but also offered information and helpful suggestions regarding the topic.

Since the wartime letters involved engagements of volunteer regiments as well as militia from both Ohio and Illinois, I felt it necessary to provide the reader with more details regarding the military context for the events described in the various letters. My goal was to provide others with enough information so that they might better understand the circumstances and emotions surrounding those at home and those at the front.

Sergeant Montgomery's great-granddaughter, Eloise Egbert, who has for many years been the guardian and keeper of this wonderful collection, made the letters and the wartime journals available to me. I am indebted to her for allowing me access to family photographs, obituaries, and newspaper accounts of family members. Eloise also introduced me to Imogene Kinley (known to family and friends as Jeanne), who was also a great granddaughter of the soldier. Both women were willing and eager to share with me their remembrances of their great-grandmother, Mary Ann Montgomery, and of the family home on Dogwood Ridge. It would have been impossible to write this book without their support and assistance. Sadly, Imogene passed away on May 19, 2010, well before the publication of this book. She was ninety-eight years old.

I am also indebted to two friends, Barbara Carl, a long-time friend from college, and Dawn Mowery, a fellow member of the Cincinnati Civil War Round Table. These women graciously agreed to read various drafts of the manuscript and to offer valuable critiques and suggestions.

I also want to acknowledge the excellent research assistance from Rebecca Livingston of Silver Spring, Maryland, who retrieved several pension and military service records for me from the National Archives.

My thanks go to Jim Christy, an artist from Rochester, New York, for his original watercolor painting of Sergeant Montgomery.

In 2009 at the Ohio Civil War show in Mansfield, Ohio, I discovered the colored pencil artwork of Amy B. Lindenberger of Gettysburg, Pennsylvania. My attention was immediately drawn to a work from her series titled "Beyond the Battlefield." It depicted a touching scene of a soldier comforting his young daughter as he was about to depart for the war. I felt that this captured the emotional impact I hope the book might convey. I am grateful to Amy for allowing me to use "A Promise to Return" for the cover of the book.

The cover design for this book, as well as for my regimental histories, is the work of the graphic design office of Mike Stretch at Steadfast Studios in Mason, Ohio. Thanks to Valerie Hoffman for designing this cover.

With this project, as with most of my others, I often encountered difficulties of a technical nature with the computer. As usual, I relied heavily upon the expertise of my son, Mark, to resolve those issues and for that he has my love and gratitude.

Despite the many problems I encountered, I was fortunate that my husband Tutt was always there to provide constant love and support for my efforts. He has also, without objection, willingly read countless versions of rewrites and offered suggestions and encouragement. He is and has always been my emotional anchor in all that I do.

# Bibliography

Ackerman, William K. *Sketch of the Illinois-Central Railroad And Biographical Record of Incorporation*. Charleston, South Carolina: Biblio Life, 2008.

Adjutant General of Ohio. *Roster of Ohio Soldiers in the War of 1812*. Baltimore, Md.: Clearfield Company Reprints & Remainders by Genealogy Publishing Company, 1989.

Adjutant-General's Office. *Roster of Wisconsin Volunteers, War of the rebellion, 1861–1865*. Madison, Wis.: Democrat Printing Co., state printers, 1886.

Barr, Daniel P., ed. *The Boundaries Between Us: Natives and Newcomers Along the Frontiers of the Old Northwest Territory, 1750–1850*. Kent, Ohio: Kent State University Press, 2006.

Bissland, James. *Blood, Tears and Glory: How Ohioans Won the Civil War*. Wilmington, Ohio: Orange Frazier Press, 2007.

Blanton, De Anne and Lauren M. Cook. *They Fought Like Demons*. Baton Rouge: Louisiana University Press, 2002.

Bonney, Edward. *The Banditti of the Prairie; The Murderer's Doom*. Chicago: Homeward Publications, 1850.

Boucher, John N and John W. Jordan. *History of Westmoreland County, Pennsylvania*. New York: Lewis Publishing Company, 1906.

Bowers, Laura Allen. "Some things I remember of Chief Shabbona." In *History of Kane County, Illinois,* by R. Waite and Frank W. Joslyn. Chicago: The Pioneer Publishing Company.

Bradsby, H. D. editor. *History of Bureau County, Illinois.* Chicago: World Publishing Company, 1885.

Brockett, L. P. *Battlefield and Hospital: Or, Light and Shadows of the Great Rebellion.* Philadelphia: Hubbard Brothers, 1888.

Clinton, Catherine. *Public Women of the Confederacy.* Milwaukee: Marquette University Press, 1999.

Cochran, Joseph. *Centennial History of Mason County: Including A Sketch of the early History of Illinois.* Springfield, Ill.: Rockers Steam Printing House, 1876.

Congdon, George Edward. *Waterman Yearbook 1904, Third Annual Volume.* Sac City, Iowa: *The Sac Sun*, 1906.

Dahl, Beverly Montgomery. "In Search of the Montgomery Mills." Mesa, Ariz.: Unpublished Manuscript, 1989.

Evans, Nelson W. *A History of Scioto County, Ohio, together With A Pioneer Record of Southern Ohio.* Portsmouth, Ohio: Nelson W. Evans, 1903.

Fletcher, Holly Berkeley. *Gender and the American Temperance Movement.* New York: Routledge, 2008.

Flood, Charles Bracelen. *1864: Lincoln at the Gates of History.* New York: Simon & Schuster, 2009.

Ford, Henry A. *The History of Putnam and Marshall Counties: Embracing an Account of the Settlement, early Progress and Formation of Bureau and Stark Counties.* Henry, Ill.: M. and D. Print Company, 1860.

Gargiulo, Barbara. *Scioto County Ohio Newspaper Index: Deaths and Marriages 1818 to 1865.* Milford, Ohio: Little Miami Publishing, 1998.

Harris, S. D. "Agriculture and Horticulture: Promotion of Domestic Industry," *Ohio Cultivator* 14 (1858).

Hatch, Luther A. *The Indian Chief Shabonna*, Dekalb, Ill.: Mrs. L. A. Hatch, 1915.

Harford, John. *It Will Never Be As It Once Was: The Private Letters of Civil War Soldier John Harford.* Princeton, Ill.: Bureau County Historical Society, 2006.

Harper, Judith E. *Women During the Civil War: An Encyclopedia,* New York: Routledge, 2004.

Harper, Robert S. *Ohio Handbook of the Civil War.* Columbus: Ohio Historical Society, 1961.

Herbert, Jeffrey G., trans., and Barbara Keyser Gargiulo, ed. *Translated Abstracts of Death Notices in the Portsmouth Correspondent, 1894–1908.* Milford, Ohio: Little Miami Publishing Company, 2000.

Hill, H. H. *History of Lee County.* Chicago: H. H. Hill Publisher, 1881.

*History of Benton County, Iowa: containing a history of the county, its cities, towns, etc.* Chicago: Western Historical Company, 1878.

*History of Logan County, Illinois: Together with Sketches of its Cities, Villages and towns, Educational, Religious, Civil Military and Political History, portraits of Prominent persons, and biographies of Representative Citizens.* Chicago: Inter-State Publishing Co, 1886.

*History of Logan County Illinois: Its past and present.* Chicago: Loyd Donnelley & Company Publishing Company, 1878.

*History of the Lower Scioto Valley, Ohio.* Chicago: Inter-State Publishing Co, 1884.

*History and Roster of Maryland Volunteers, War of 1861–5.* Vol. I Prepared under authority of The General Assembly of Maryland by L. Allison Wilmer, J. H. Jarrett, Geo. W. F. Vernon, State Commissioners. Baltimore, Md.: Press of Guggenheimer, Weil & Co., *1898.*

Hubin, Allen. *Crime Fiction IV: A Comprehensive Bibliography 1749–2000.* Oakland Calif.: Locus Press, 2008.

Howe, Henry. *Historical Collections of Ohio in Two Volumes.* Cincinnati, Ohio: C. J. Krehbiel & Co. Printers and Binders, 1902.

Hurd, Harvey Bostwick and Robert Dickinson Sheppard. *Historical Encyclopedia of Illinois.* p. 566, Chicago: Middle West Publishing Company, 1906.

Hurt, R. Douglas. *The Ohio Frontier: Crucible of the Old Northwest. 1720– 1830.* Bloomington: Indiana University Press, 1996.

——— and Howard R. Lamar, David J. Weber, William Cronon, and Martin Ridge, eds. *The Indian Frontier: 1763–1786.* Albuquerque: University of New Mexico Press, 1997.

Janes, Albina, Obituary. *Bureau County Record,* from collection of Eloise Egbert, Lucasville, Ohio. Princeton, Ill.: Bureau County Press, September 1910.

Joslyn, R. Waite and Frank W. Joslyn. *History of Kane County, Illinois,* Chicago: The Pioneer Publishing , 1908.

Keyes, James. *Pioneers of Scioto County: Being a Short Biographical Sketch of some of the First Settlers of Scioto County, Ohio.* Columbus, Ohio: Walsworth Publishing Co, 1880.

Kirkland, Frazier. *Pictorial Book of Anecdotes and Incidents of The War of the Rebellion,* 1866. Philadelphia Pa.: Hurlburt, Williams & Co., 1889.

Knepper, George. *Ohio and its People.* Kent, Ohio: Kent State University Press, 2003.

Lambert, Lois J. *Heroes of the Western Theater: Thirty-third Ohio Veteran Volunteer Infantry.* Milford, Ohio: Little Miami Publishing, 2008.

Larkin, Jack. *The Reshaping of Everyday Life: 1790–1840.* New York: Harper & Rowe, 1988.

Leeke, Richard. *A Hundred Days to Richmond: Ohio's "Hundred Days" Men in the Civil War.* Bloomington: Indiana University Press, 1997.

Martin, James and A. Kristen Foster, eds. *More Than a Contest Between Armies: Essays on the Civil War Era.* Kent, Ohio: Kent State University Press, 2009.

Massey, Mary Elizabeth. *Bonnet Brigades* (The Impact of the Civil War Series). New York: Alfred A. Knopf, 1966.

Matson, Nehemiah. *Maps and Sketches of Bureau County, Illinois.* Princeton, Ill.: Bureau County Illinois Historical Society, 1867.

———. *Memories of Shaubena.* Princeton, Ill.: Bureau County Illinois Historical Society, 1878.

McNitt, Francina. Obituary from unidentified 1915 Illinois newspaper. Collection of Eloise Egbert, Lucasville, Ohio.

McShane, Clay and Joel A. Tarr: *The Horse in the City, Living Machines in the Nineteenth Century.* Baltimore, Md.: Johns Hopkins University Press, 2007.

Montgomery, John S. "Venerable Citizen of Bureau County, One of the Early Settlers, Passes Away, Age 87." Obituary, 1907 Unidentified Illinois newspaper from collection of Eloise Egbert, Lucasville, Ohio.

Hamilton, Stanislaus Murray, ed. *The Writings of James Monroe, Including a Collection of His Public and Private Papers and Correspondence, Vol. I.*, New York: G. P. Putnam's Sons, 1898.

Murphy, Edward. *Shabbona: Friend of the White Man.* Lockport, Ill.: Will County Historical Society, 1981.

Ohio History: The Scholarly Journal of the Ohio Historical Society, Vol. 64. Agricultural Report for 1857, Columbus, Ohio: Ohio Historical Society, 1955.

*Ohio State Parks Magazine: "Ohio's Iron Age."* Columbus, Ohio: Ohio Department of Natural Resources, Fall 2009– Winter 2010.

Pooley, William Vipond. *Settlement of Illinois from 1830–1850.* Madison: University of Wisconsin, 1905.

Ramage, James A. *Rebel Raider: The Life of General John Hunt Morgan.* Lexington: The University of Kentucky Press, 1986.

Reid, Whitelaw. *Ohio in the War: Her Statesmen, her Generals, and Soldiers.* vols. 1 and 2. Cincinnati, Ohio: Moore, Wilstach & Baldwin, 1868.

*Report of the Adjutant General of the State of Indiana.* vol. 3, 1861–1865. Indianapolis, Ind.: Samuel A. Douglas, State printer, 1866.

Ridgley, Douglas C. *Geography of Illinois.* Chicago: The University of Chicago Press, 1921.

Rist, Donald E. *Iron Furnaces of the Hanging Rock Region.* Signal Mountain, Tenn.: Waldenhouse Publishers, Inc., 1974.

Roberts, William H. *Civil War Ironclads: The U.S. Navy and Industrial Mobilization*. Baltimore, Md.: Johns Hopkins University Press, 2002.

Roster Commission. *Official Roster of the Soldiers of the State of Ohio in the War of the Rebellion, 1861–1866, Vol. IV, 37st–53rd Regiments-Infantry*. Cincinnati, Ohio: Published by The Ohio Valley Press under the Authority of the General Assembly, 1888.

———. *Official Roster of the Soldiers of the State of Ohio in the War of the Rebellion, 1861–1866, Vol. III, 21st–36th Regiments-Infantry*. Cincinnati, Ohio: The Ohio Valley Press under the Authority of the General Assembly, 1888.

*Sangamon County, Illinois: Together with Sketches of its Cities, Villages and Township, Educational, religious, Civil, Military and Political History*. Chicago: Interstate Publishing Company, 1881.

Shoemaker, Caryn R. Fuller and Betty J. Sisler Rudity. *Marriage Records of Scioto County, Ohio 1803–1860*. Baltimore, Md.: Genealogical Publishing Company, 1987.

Stevens, Frank Everett. *The Black Hawk War: Including A Review of Black Hawk's Life*. Chicago: Frank E. Wright Publisher, 1903.

Stevens, Frank Everett. *History of Lee County, Illinois*. Chicago: S. J. Clarke Publishing Co., 1914.

Temple, Wayne C. *Shabbona, Friend of the Whites*. Springfield, Ill. Illinois State Museum, 1957.

U.S. War Department. A *Compilation of the Official Records of the Union and Confederate Armies*. 128 vols. Washington, D.C.: Government Printing Office, 1880–1900.

Volker, Lowell M. transcription and index. *Illinois Mortality Schedule 1850– Vol. I, Counties Adams through Iroquois*. Indianapolis, Indiana: Volker, n.d.

Welcher, Frank J. *The Union Army 1861–1865: Organization And Operations Volume II: The Western Theater*. Bloomington and Indianapolis, Ind.: Indiana University Press, 1989.

Williard, Eugene B., Daniel W. Williams, and George O. Newman, eds. *A Standard History of the Hanging Rock Iron Region*. Cleveland, Ohio: The Lewis Publishing Company, 1916.

Wyman, Mark. *Immigrants in the Valley: Irish, Germans, and Americans in the Upper Mississippi Country, 1830–1860*. Chicago: Nelson Hall Publisher, 1984.

Young, John Preston. *A Standard History of Memphis Tennessee*. Knoxville, Tenn.: H. W. Crew and Company, 1912.

## INTERNET SOURCES

Ancestry.com. "1890 Veterans Schedules" [database online by subscription]. Provo, Utah. Original data: United States of America, Bureau of the Census. Special Schedules of the Eleventh Census (1890) enumerating Union Veterans and Widows of Union veterans of the Civil War. Washington, D.C.: National Archives and Records Administration, 1890. (accessed between June 5 through September 4, 2009).

———. Federal Census 1850–1910 [database online by subscription]. Provo, Utah. Original data: United States of America, Bureau of the Census. Original data: United States of America, Bureau of the Census. Washington, D.C.: National Archives and Records Administration. (accessed between June 5 through September 4, 2009).

Illinois Civil War Muster and Description Rolls, Illinois State Archives online database. http://www.ilsos.gov/genealogy/index.jsp. (accessed September 4–24, 2009).

Illinois State Journal; Chicago Press and Tribune. *'Incidents at Ottawa'* in the *'Illinois State Journal.'* Springfield: Bailhache and Baker, 1858. University of Chicago. NIU Libraries Digitization Projects. http://lincoln.lib.niu.edu/cgi-bin/philologic/navigate.pl?lincoln 2191 (accessed September 4, 2009).

Ohio History Central on line, "Cholera Epidemics" http://www.ohiohistorycentral.org/entry.php?rec=487 (accessed July 8, 2009).

Ohio Historical Society. The Ohio Historical Society Civil War documents searchable database. ohiohistory.org/resource/database/ civilwar.html (accessed June 11, 2009)

## MANUSCRIPTS

Civil War letters, diary, and artifacts of Sergeant McLain Montgomery, Company A, Thirty-third Ohio Infantry. 1861–1864. Eloise Egbert Collection, Lucasville, Ohio.

Civil War letters of Private George W. Montgomery, Company A, Thirty-ninth Ohio Infantry. 1862–1863. Eloise Egbert Collection, Lucasville, Ohio. Civil War letters of members of the Montgomery family from Bureau County, Illinois, regarding Thirty-first Illinois Volunteer Infantry and Sixty-fourth Illinois Volunteer Infantry. 1862–1863. Eloise Egbert Collection, Lucasville, Ohio.

Civil War letters of Angus Waddle, 1862–1864. Eleanor Waddle McCoy Collection, Missouri Historical Society Archives, St. Louis, Missouri.

Prewar letters from McLain Montgomery and Isaac Newton Montgomery from Bureau County, Illinois. 1853-1856. Eloise Egbert Collection, Lucasville, Ohio.

Pension and Compiled Military Service Records of individual soldiers from the Montgomery family of Scioto County, Ohio, and Bureau County, Illinois. National Archives and Records Administration, Washington, D.C.

# Index